Being Brave

A 40-Day Journey to the Life God Dreams for You

Kelly Johnson

ABINGDON PRESS
Nashville

BEING BRAVE
A 40-DAY JOURNEY TO THE LIFE GOD DREAMS FOR YOU

Library of Congress Cataloging-in-Publication Data

Names: Johnson, Kelly (Kelly Ivey), author.
Title: Being brave : a forty-day journey to the life God dreams for you / Kelly Johnson.
Description: Nashville : Abingdon Press, [2017] | Includes bibliographical references and index.
Identifiers: LCCN 2017034471 (print) | LCCN 2017039748 (ebook) | ISBN 9781501848667 (ebook) | ISBN 9781501848650 (pbk. : alk. paper)
Subjects: LCSH: Christian women—Conduct of life. | Women—Conduct of life. | Lent—Prayers and devotions.
Classification: LCC BV4527 (ebook) | LCC BV4527 .J6364 2017 (print) | DDC 248.8/43--dc23
LC record available at https://urldefense.proofpoint.com/v2/url?u=https-3A__lccn.loc.gov_2017034471&d=DwIFAg&c=_GnokDXYZpxapTjbCjzmOH7Lm2x2J46Ijwz6YxXCKeo&r=ox0wiE5wyq1D4NWBvXI_LEW57Ah1_xv-dTElReAYRyw&m=xK_1LUa_I0II4JM9YHVUX2cF5n0TvH6PJUvK0-3sTDo&s=iDnlJRXXBWSUz_yI_rrzi2eLFxoN7e7y8YCNVvcL_So&e=

17 18 19 20 21 22 23 24 25 26—10 9 8 7 6 5 4 3 2 1

MANUFACTURED IN THE UNITED STATES OF AMERICA

Praise for *Being Brave*

"Kelly Johnson leads us through a forty-day journey of living boldly through the power of the Holy Spirit. She offers thought-provoking stories and questions that are sure to get you thinking about bravery in a fresh way. This beautiful devotional journey is inspiring and uplifting." —**Micah Maddox**, author of *Anchored In*

"In *Being Brave*, Kelly Johnson invites us to stop settling for safe and instead embrace who we were created to be by the God who loves us. This means setting aside fear, distrust, and the masks we wear for self-protection in favor of courage, authenticity, and trust in the Lord. Kelly's gentle but firm exhortations to be brave, and her confidence that we all have it in us to do just that, will lead you on a forty-day journey to a more fulfilled, more engaged, truer you." —**Harmony Harkema**, *The Glorious Table*

"Culture shouts: 'Be brave! Power through life fearlessly!' Kelly Johnson turns this notion upside down by tapping into Christ's definition of *brave*: His strength made perfect in our weakness. Her vulnerable struggles and victories move me to live with more honesty, grace, love, and joy." —**Christina Hubbard**, author of *Five Ways To Love Like You Mean It* and founder of CreativeandFree.com

"Kelly Johnson does a beautiful job of opening our eyes to the One who makes us Brave. Each forty-day encounter with God through His Word ends with engaging questions and prayer, which bring us to deepen our resolve in our walk with Him." —**Becky Shaffer**, Executive Director, Saving Grace NWA

"Kelly Johnson is willing to take an honest look at her life and tackle tough topics like cynicism, fear, and discontent to help us uncover what may be holding us back in our own lives. This book in insightful and encouraging and will inspire you to bravely step into the life God has planned for you!" —**Sue Bidstrup**, founder of Great Big Yes!, www.greatbigyes.com

"In a world of struggle over prejudice, comparison, anxiety, sentimentality, perfectionism, and injustice of all kinds, this is just the prescription we all need. Pick up this book and stop. Breathe. Rest. Reflect. Pray. By the end of your spiritual journey you will find yourself rolling up your sleeves empowered to join God's movement again. Be Bold. Be Brave. Be Church." —**Dr. Tobin E. Wilson**, pastor, author, and thought leader

"Kelly Johnson enables us to see the important link between courage and a faith that responds to God's calling in daily life. Reading *Being Brave* made me see opportunities to take risks for Jesus, to have courage and encourage others. Only when we are brave will we find the fullness of life in Christ." —**Rev. Tom Berlin**, Floris United Methodist Church

"Through *Being Brave*, Kelly Johnson guides us one day at a time to live full and free from the lies that keep us from trusting that God is enough, releasing us to make the difference we were born to make." —**Elisa Johnston**, author and founder of Average Advocate

"*Being Brave* wholly encouraged me to see the brave in myself and emboldened me to call out the brave in others. This devotional will surely move you to live more passionately in the abundance and self-worth found in Christ!" —**Courtney Westlake**, author of *A Different Beautiful*

"Day after day, I'd pick up *Being Brave* to find Kelly's words speaking directly to my life. Her insights and stories are relevant, impactful, and beautifully written. I finished the book feeling strong and capable of facing whatever God put in front of me, and then I handed it to my teenage daughter." —**Katy Epling**, writer and speaker

"Kelly's writing feels like good conversation with a wise and fun friend who gets you. I found myself nodding along so much, I eventually gave up on highlighting and just circled entire pages writing, '*This!*' Her vulnerable style offers a welcome 'me too' as she invites us all to call out the best in one another and ourselves." —**Melinda Mattson**, writer and speaker

"For anyone feeling overcome by limitations and fear, Kelly Johnson names us brave and gives us the tools to step into our fullest potential. Kelly's words are wise, insightful, and relatable. The questions in each chapter help get beyond the surface to the root of fear." —**Kelly Smith**, writer at MrsDisciple.com

"Being Brave is everything your mother forgot to tell you about summoning bravery when it's needed most. Wise, grace-filled, funny, and just plain 'spot-on,' this devotional will stir your heart and spur you onward. I didn't know I needed to be named brave, but now I know I'll never be the same." —**Stacey Philpot**, writer and advocate

"I used to believe that I was the one that had to be brave, but in the last year I learned that God makes us brave; He gives us all we need to be bold, be vulnerable, and embrace the best He has for us! Kelly's book is full of truth and scripture to remind us daily not to fall back into the darkness of lies. If you have felt that you aren't brave enough, then this devotional will revive the spark inside your soul!" —**Tara Royer Steele**, The Brave Gathering

For Steve,
You are my greatest blessing
and my heart is yours forever.
Your love makes me brave.

For Alexandra and Brooke,
Always remember you are brave warriors
and beloved daughters of the King.
Be good, be strong, be brave!

Together, we remember that we are brave!

Blessings –

Kelly

Contents

Introduction ix

PART 1: POWER 1

Being Brave Is Being *Bold* 3

Being Brave Is Being *Resilient* 23

PART 2: LOVE 49

Being Brave Is Being *Authentic* 51

Being Brave Is Being *Vulnerable* 77

PART 3: SELF-DISCIPLINE 103

Being Brave Is Being *Engaged* 105

Being Brave Is Being *Empowered* by the Spirit 131

Being Brave Invitation from God 159

Scriptures About Fear and Courage 161

Introduction

Our Journey with Brave

I am not an expert on being brave. I don't have a secret treasure map, a magic wand, or five easy steps that lead to bravery. However, for the last several years, I have considered myself a student of what being brave looks like—a brave aficionado, a connoisseur of courage. I've become a collector of clues to a deeper understanding of brave and a rabble-rouser inviting others to join the cause.

The journey began when my daughter ignited my curiosity around the word *brave* and changed the way we looked at life going forward.

When my youngest daughter, Brooke, was nine, she was having a particularly difficult day. Always a worrier and prone to processing every thought out loud, she found the world especially overwhelming that day. I couldn't seem to find a way to help her get to the other side of her increasing angst. She had worn me out with her growing list of worries, complaints, aches, pains, and fears, and I told her I didn't know what else I could do for her. Whatever it was, I couldn't fix it. I had no more answers; I was done.

Sensing my frustration, she looked at me with her big blue eyes filled with tears and said the words that have continued to be our mantra to one another: "Mommy, I just need you to tell me I'm a brave soldier."

And so I did. As she grew up and faced down some increasingly difficult circumstances, I said those words over and over until she learned to claim them for herself. Naming her brave and affirming her courage allowed her to access an inner strength previously just out of reach. As a young adult, she has continued to surround herself with people who are similarly willing to encourage and affirm her hard-won courage. For her nineteenth birthday, I gave her a bracelet with the words *Be Brave* etched into a silver cuff—a tangible symbol of my words to her when I am too far away to speak them out loud. I wear an identical bracelet as a reminder that I too am capable of courage.

Naming one another brave has become the way we offer encouragement in our family, our special language of love. We have expanded our circle of courage by naming our friends brave as well. Within our inner circle, naming one another BRAVE, calling out the *brave soldier* in one another, is our way of speaking out loud the following message of solidarity and inspiration:

I see your struggle; I see your brave, hard work.
I believe in you, and I'm here if you need help.

When I look up the definition of *brave* in the dictionary, I find these words: "Ready to face and endure danger or pain; showing courage. As in 'a brave soldier.' " It makes me smile to see the dictionary writer's chosen example to illustrate and encapsulate the word *brave*: an example that has become so much a part of our daily parlance.

Being brave means something different to all of us. We would all agree that a person on a battlefield requires a large degree of bravery. Facing a diagnosis of cancer or sitting with the pain of losing someone you love requires great courage as well. However, the need for bravery is not always black and white. What might be terrifying or hard for some might be easy for others. When I think about the times I need to dig deep for courage, I find the danger is sometimes more perception than reality.

The scariest things for me are often risking vulnerability and allowing myself to be seen as inadequate. I am scared of the unknown, of loss, of change, of that which I can't control, of making a fool of myself, and of not being able to protect those I love. Is being brave in those circumstances even related to the kind of bravery required to lay down your life in a combat zone? What does this other kind of everyday courage look like? And who or what is the source of that courage?

When Brooke left for college a few years ago and I was faced with the prospect of my newly empty nest, I began to dig more deeply into this concept of being brave and what it might mean in this season of transition. Talking to my friends who faced similar challenges, I found a number of similarities in the ways we chose courage over fear.

Being brave might include any or all of the following:

- Being willing to move forward, even when I'm scared.
- Living creatively, chasing my dreams, and not settling for safe.
- Being driven more by my curiosity than by my fears.
- Being vulnerable and authentic in my relationships, even though I can't control the outcome.
- Trusting other people, even though I have been hurt.
- Being honest about who I am and what I want.

- Admitting when I am wrong and taking responsibility for my mistakes.
- Taking risks and being willing to fail.
- Asking for help.
- Believing my story is an important part of the larger story God is telling.
- Embracing progress, not perfection.

God Names Us Brave

The transformational power of being named brave originates with God. It is no secret to our creator that His children struggle with fear and doubt. Knowing we would need reminders of the bravery He has placed within us, Scripture is replete with encouragement from God in our hunt for the courage we need to live the abundant lives He has planned for us. Repeatedly, God says, "Fear not!" in a myriad of ways. It is one of the most frequent commands in the Bible. (At the end of the book is a list of some of the many verses in Scripture about fear and courage.) In every case, God's call for courage is connected to His presence. We can be brave because God is always with us.

In 2 Timothy 1:7, the apostle Paul reminds his spiritual son Timothy that courage is his birthright as a child of God: "For God has not given us a spirit of fear and timidity, but of power, love, and self-discipline" (NLT).

Throughout our forty-day journey, we will return repeatedly to this verse as our theme. In this verse, Paul reminds Timothy that God has given us all we need to live a life of courage through the power of the Holy Spirit. Because of Jesus, we have access to a spirit of power, love, and self-control. Although God has given us all we need to be brave, many of us forget and find ourselves stuck in discouragement, fearfulness, and inaction. We play it safe when God wants us to be bold, and we hide from one another when God wants us to live in community. Being brave is our inheritance as children of God, and being brave is the path to a life of meaning, purpose, and adventure. Through our connection to one another and to God, we learn to tackle our greatest fears and move closer to realizing our dreams. Together, we remember we are brave.

How to Use This Book

Over the next forty days, I invite you to join me on a journey to uncover the seeds of divinely inspired bravery God has placed within each one of us. We will dig deeper into our theme verse by considering how this life-giving spirit can make a difference in the way we choose to live. Each day, we will meditate on two additional verses, and I will share stories about the ways God has shown me a different way of thinking about being brave in my own life and in the lives of the people around me. On our journey, we will look for inspiration from Jesus and His closest followers during the final weeks of His earthly ministry, powerful examples of the various components of courage we will be exploring. Farther down the road, I will also introduce you to some of the bravest people I know—my friends at The Lamb Center, a day shelter for homeless and poor individuals in my community.

To help us understand the building blocks of being brave, we will look through the lens of a BRAVE acronym:

Bold
Resilient
Authentic
Vulnerable
Engaged

And, saving the best for last, we consider the ways in which the Holy Spirit offers us the fuel for our brave journey with a bonus *E* word, Empowered by the Spirit. Using our theme verse in combination with the BRAVE acronym, our journey is divided into three sections.

God's Spirit of Power = Being Bold and Resilient
God's Spirit of Love = Being Authentic and Vulnerable
God's Spirit of Self-Discipline = Being Engaged and Empowered by the Spirit

I encourage you to read the chosen Scriptures before reading the accompanying devotion. Using a special notebook or journal, spend some time reflecting on the questions at the end of each day's selection. Answer all three questions or choose one that particularly speaks to you. Use the concluding prayer to begin a conversation with God about how the concept you explored that day applies to your unique situation, listening for the ways He invites you to take the next step in your journey.

Are you ready to be brave? Let's dig in!

PART 1

Power

For God has not given us a spirit of fear and timidity, but of POWER, love, and self-discipline.

—2 Timothy 1:7 NLT

Power is defined as "the ability to act or produce an effect." When we embrace our power, we believe we can make change happen in ourselves and in our world. Although our theme verse tells us God has given each of us a spirit of power, many of us feel stuck or powerless in some area of our life. In some cases, our circumstances or responsibilities contribute to us feeling stuck, but in many cases, something about our inner dialogue keeps us from fully realizing the life we desire. Our inner critic speaks the language of lies and perpetuates the myth that causes us to cling to our identity of powerlessness. To experience the *dunamis,* or resurrection power God offers to us, we need to decide who we will allow to name us: God or the voices who want to keep us stuck in the safety of the status quo. In this section, we will explore what it means to be *bold* and *resilient,* fully connected to the power of God's Spirit and capable of being the change we wish to see in the world.

Being Brave Is Being Bold

Day 1

Yes, be bold and strong! Banish fear and doubt! For remember, the Lord your God is with you wherever you go.

—Joshua 1:9 TLB

Therefore, since we have such a hope, we are very bold.

—2 Corinthians 3:12

Being brave is being bold.

Bold means "showing an ability to take risks, confident, and courageous." When I consider the word *bold,* I think of people who are willing to speak up for themselves or take charge of a situation. Bold behavior comes from a sense of personal power and may in some cases indicate a willingness to be in a position of authority. Some words synonymous with bold might include *daring, intrepid, valiant, fearless, dauntless, audacious, spunky, feisty, spirited,* and *gutsy.*

Unlike some of the other brave words we will be exploring in the coming weeks, *bold* doesn't always have completely positive connotations. Bold is also sometimes used to describe a person who is presumptuous, impudent, or impertinent. A bold person, for better or worse, is not afraid to break the rules of propriety, if needed. A person who is gutsy might in some cases be seen as overstepping boundaries or taking things too far. What some might call audacious, others might see as bordering on rude.

For women, the expectations around being bold can be even more confusing. A woman who is bold might be seen as being arrogantly overconfident or lacking in humility. She may be described as bratty, brash, pushy, and demanding.

And therein lies the dilemma.

We are sometimes reluctant to be bold for fear of being perceived as difficult.

Or rude. Or pushy. Or too much trouble. Or presumptuous. Or whatever other word we associate with taking up too much space in the world.

Boldness is often confronted with the question: "Just who do you think you are?"

God's word offers guidance on this issue of boldness in our Scriptures for today. Being bold in these Scriptures is associated with our proximity to divine presence. By virtue of our faith and trust in God, we are secure and made brave. We rest in God's love and protection, and, in Him, we find our unique voice and learn to use it wisely. Because we learn to use our voice under the guidance of the Holy Spirit, we know when to speak up and when to choose silence instead. We learn to speak the truth in love, balancing clear communication with kindness and compassion. As we explore God's definition of boldness, we find courage and confidence we didn't know we had.

Boldness, in God's economy, is the answer to the question "*Whose* do you think you are?"

Because we belong to God, our place is secure. Because we are completely loved, we can be assured of our right and perhaps even our responsibility to speak up and be heard. Boldness gives us the confidence to step out of our comfort zone and take a risk, knowing there is someone to catch us if we fall. Boldness gives us the courage to accept God's invitation for more, even when we are still scared.

As Sigmund Freud once said, "How bold one gets when one is sure of being loved."

Being bold is part of being brave.

1. What does the word *bold* mean to you? On first reflection, does it have more positive or negative connotations for you?
2. Can you think of situations in which you have been willing to be bold?
3. In what areas would you like to be bolder?

Prayer: Father, help us be curious this week as we consider what it means to be bold. Give us faith in our wondering and open our minds and hearts to consider what boldness might mean to You and how it applies to our lives. Remind us of Your perfect love for us and, as we rest in that love, nudge us forward in our brave journey. We are excited to hear from You, Lord! Thank You for Your word and the examples of the ordinary people in the pages of our Bible who lived lives of boldness and courage. Amen.

Day 2

Because of Christ and our faith in him, we can now come boldly and confidently into God's presence.

—Ephesians 3:12 NLT

See what great love the Father has lavished on us, that we should be called children of God! And that is what we are!

—1 John 3:1

When my younger daughter was in her teens, she put together a PowerPoint presentation to convince her father to let her pierce a second hole in her ears. Personally, I didn't care how many holes she had in her ears, but our parenting policy had always been to present a united front behind the opinion of whoever felt the most strongly. In this case, Steve was convinced a second hole was a gateway to multiple piercings, unsightly tattoos, and a life of crime. As I watched her make her case, I chuckled quietly to myself, knowing full well he was destined to lose his resolve to his determined daughter.

From the time they were tiny, our girls knew it was safe to go to their big, strong daddy with the desires of their heart. Although he sometimes had to say no because he knew root beer floats for dinner or a ride to the mall with a newly driving friend wasn't in their best interests, he always listened to their requests and delighted in the times he could say yes. From the minute they walked into the room saying, "Daddy, please," he would light up with pleasure at their presence. Whether climbing into his lap when they were little or scooting up under his open arm as they grew bigger, they knew they were welcome, loved, and safe. They grew up believing their voice mattered because their daddy listened when they spoke. Because of these beginnings, they are strong young women who are comfortable speaking up boldly and confidently about those things that matter most to them. They trust their voice and believe it matters.

This image of a little girl confident in her daddy's love is what comes to mind when I read today's verses. Because we are completely loved, we can boldly and confidently pour out our hearts to our heavenly Father. While many of us did not have this kind of relationship with our earthly father, Jesus has paved the way for all of us to have this kind of access to our Father above. Throughout the Gospels, we know Jesus cherished the time He spent talking to His Father about the desires of His heart. Jesus prioritized His time in prayer and encouraged His followers to do the same. Jesus sets the example for us of a relationship with God characterized by consistent and continual conversation.

Because our God chose us as His own, we can be confident He wants to hear what we have to say: the complaints, the worries, the hurts, the joys, the fears, and the dreams. We don't have to measure our words or use any kind of special prayer language. We can simply speak from the heart because it brings God pleasure to call us His children.

Our Scripture today reminds us of the generosity and extravagance of the way God loves us. Just like my daughters with their daddy, we can run into our Father's presence and talk openly and honestly about our lives, knowing we will be greeted with delight. Because we know God hears us, we know our voice is valued. When we truly believe that our voice matters, we become braver about trusting our voice in the world.

1. What kind of relationship did you have with your earthly father? How has this impacted your perception of God as your heavenly Father, either positively or negatively?
2. Do you believe you can talk to God about anything? Why or why not?
3. When it comes to your relationships with other people, do you find it easy or difficult to ask for what you want? Why is asking for what you want important in our journey to be brave?

Prayer: Heavenly Father, heal any wounds that may be left behind by a complicated relationship with our earthly father. Teach us to call You Abba Father, which means "Daddy." Help us to trust Your voice and know You have only our good in mind in every situation. When we forget, remind us we are safe with You and that You delight in our presence each time we run into Your warm, welcoming embrace. Thank You for lavishing us with Your extravagant love and for listening to us whenever we turn to You. Amen.

Day 3

When the Council saw the boldness of Peter and John and could see that they were obviously uneducated non-professionals, they were amazed and realized what being with Jesus had done for them!

—Acts 4:13 TLB

He pressed them, "And how about you? Who do you say I am?"

Simon Peter said, "You're the Christ, the Messiah, the Son of the living God."

Jesus came back, "God bless you, Simon, son of Jonah! You didn't get that answer out of books or from teachers. My Father in heaven, God himself, let you in on this secret of who I really am. And now I'm going to tell you who you are, really are. You are Peter, a rock. This is the rock on which I will put together my church, a church so expansive with energy that not even the gates of hell will be able to keep it out."

—Matthew 16:15-18 MSG

Many of us were taught to choose our friends carefully because of the often-repeated truth, "You are the company you keep." For those of us who love or parent children, we hold our breath and watch with greater vigilance when we see that child entering into a relationship with a peer we fear might not be the best influence. Right or wrong, we know we are often judged by the behavior of those with whom we choose to spend our time.

Another way our friends influence us is the way they name us. We tend to internalize the messages, both verbal and nonverbal, we receive from our loved ones. The friend who says, "You are such a good mom," offers much needed encouragement on those days when our kids are on our very last nerve and we are about to lose it again. The coworker who tells us how much he or she appreciates our excellent writing skills can make all the difference as we dig deep to finish the newsletter on time. When we share the heavy weight of our fears and doubts with our trusted friend, and she says, "You are wise and loving, and I know you will make the right choice," we have the resolve to jump back in and face our difficult circumstance with renewed strength.

We need to be thoughtful and intentional about whom we allow to name us.

As in the story about my daughter asking me to name her brave, we would be wise to surround ourselves with those who name us well. In our Scripture verses today, the council is astonished by how boldly Peter and John speak about their faith, and they attribute the courage they have witnessed to the time these men have spent with Jesus. Jesus rubbed off on His beloved disciples and He named them well. He told Peter he was the rock on which the church would be built. John was so certain about how much Jesus loved him that he refers to himself as "the one who Jesus loved" throughout the Gospel he wrote. Jesus named Peter "strong," and He named John "beloved." Despite their human frailties, Jesus told them they would do great things and He charged them with a brave mission. Jesus named them well, and, as a result, they became bold, outspoken champions for the gospel. They lived up to their names because they trusted the One who named them.

Just like the disciples with whom Jesus lived and worked during His time on earth, we have the opportunity to listen to the ways in which Jesus names us and to allow Him to change us by His presence and proximity. Like Peter and John, the more time we spend with Jesus, the more we will see ourselves through His eyes. He calls us each "beloved" and promises to be with us forever. May we be so bold that someone will say of us, "She has been hanging out with Jesus!"

1. What are the ways your friends name you well? How has that encouraged you in the past?
2. What are some ways you name others well? Can you think of a couple of ways you might be intentional about naming your loved ones well this week?
3. How does hanging out with Jesus change you? Does it make you braver? What names does Jesus call you?

Prayer: Lord, thank You for naming us beloved, forgiven, redeemed daughters of the king. Let us never forget the names You have given to us when our inner critic and the world try to convince us otherwise. Remind us to be an encourager and one who names others well. Give us courage and resolve to surround ourselves with those who see our strength and courage and call out the best in us. Help us draw closer to You in such a way that others will know we have spent time with Jesus. Amen.

Day 4

On the day I called, You answered me;
You made me bold with strength in my soul.

—Psalm 138:3 NASB

He will not be afraid of bad news. His heart is strong because he trusts in the Lord.

—Psalm 112:7 NLV

Many years ago, when I was a young mother of toddlers, I found a lump in my breast. An exam led to an ultrasound. Still not certain, the doctor ordered a biopsy. As I lay on the table trying not to watch while they cut away the tissue needed for the test, I remember thinking, "Lord, please don't let me be sick. My girls are so little. They need their mommy. Please don't take me away from my girls."

The doctor assured me I would have the results within two days. I attempted to go on with my life as I anxiously awaited the news. After the predicted two days, I called the doctor requesting results. They still did not have them available but promised I would hear from them "soon."

Three days eventually turned into a week, and I became more and more afraid. Lying awake one long night, tossing and turning, I cried out to God, "Lord, please. I just need to *know*!"

As I lay there pleading for answers, I began to sense God's presence in a deeper way. Deep in my spirit, I knew God was there and I knew

He heard me. As I continued to tell God the fears in my heart, I began to sense His calming voice saying, "Everyone will be okay. Even if you are sick, you will be okay, your husband will be okay, and your kids will be okay. Even if the worst happens, I will be with you and I will never leave you. I will be with your husband, and I will never leave him. I love your girls even more than you do, and even if you are not there, I will be there and they will be okay. I am right here and I hear you. Whatever happens, I am here."

I woke the next morning with a sense of peace and calm I had not experienced since the day I found the lump. While I was still concerned, the heaviness on my heart had been lifted, and the impending results no longer occupied my every thought. The yes or no test results were no longer my singular focus, because I had gotten an answer to a deeper question. I knew God heard my prayers and would make me brave. Whatever the news, I had confidence I was not alone.

Within twenty-four hours, I heard back from the doctor. The biopsy was negative, and I had nothing to fear. Strangely enough, the test results ended up being somewhat anticlimactic. I knew even in the midst of my fear, God was real. Whatever I faced, God would be with me. The knowledge God heard me, loved me, and promised never to leave me gave me a "strength in my soul" I have turned to many times.

Prayer is not a panacea that instantly takes away our fears. In fact, I sometimes find prayer to be awkward and unwieldy. Some days, even after years of talking to God, it feels as if my prayers are bouncing off the walls, and I wonder if I am wasting time talking to the air. Other times, like the night I describe above, God's presence and power are as tangible and real as anything I have ever experienced. When I show up in prayer consistently, whether I feel God's presence or not, I am confident God is honoring my trust in Him and building my faith. Investing in the practice of prayer, regardless of my feelings, makes my heart strong.

1. Have you ever had an experience where you cried out to God and knew He heard you?
2. If so, how did that experience change you going forward? Did it make you braver the next time life got scary?
3. When do you most often experience a sense of God's presence? What are the practices or circumstances that regularly allow you to feel connected to God?

Prayer: Lord, let us know You hear us when we cry out to You. Draw us close and give us a deeper experience of Your presence amid the challenges of our lives. Remind us we can always turn to You for answers and for a peace that passes understanding. Show us You are real in a tangible way as we turn to You with all our worries and fears. Remind us to keep praying, even on the days when our prayers seem to be bouncing off the walls. As we learn to trust You, we grow stronger day by day. Amen.

Day 5

Instead, speaking the truth in love, we will grow to become in every respect the mature body of him who is the head, that is, Christ.

—*Ephesians 4:15*

Be strong and brave. Don't be afraid of them and don't be frightened, because the Lord *your God will go with you. He will not leave you or forget you.*

—*Deuteronomy 31:6 NCV*

Several years ago, I was serving in leadership at my church and found myself feeling torn about how to respond to a particular situation. An issue under discussion concerned important denominational issues about which many of us felt strongly. As the situation unfolded, many on our board clearly assumed we all agreed with the majority opinion. As I listened, I grew more uncomfortable with the direction the conversation was heading. I disagreed vehemently, but I knew my opinion would be unpopular, so I was hesitant about sharing my thoughts. Eventually, after praying about it and mustering my courage, I decided to speak up for the benefit of those in the congregation who felt as I did. I was, after all, called to represent them in my role as a leader. I shared my opinion and found others had also been struggling in silence. My choosing to speak up gave others the courage to voice their concerns, and the conversation going forward included a more multifaceted perspective.

Whether an issue in the larger community, a situation at work, or a relationship with close friends or family, finding the courage to speak up during conflict can be difficult. Instead of dealing with a disagreement directly, we might revert to passive or indirect communication, hoping the other person will read our mind and change his or her behavior without us asking for what we need. In other cases, we find ourselves saying yes when we would prefer to say no in an attempt to keep the peace and be liked by others. Or perhaps we pretend all is fine up to the point at which our frustration boils over and we explode in anger.

Keeping my thoughts and opinions to myself is often the easier choice, so sometimes I choose the path of least resistance. In other situations, I feel the nudge in my spirit to be brave and know this is one of those times when remaining silent is not an option.

Saying no, asking for what we need, or expressing difficult feelings or opinions make us feel vulnerable. However, while it is always prudent to choose our battles prayerfully and wisely, some issues are worthy of our input, even when it is uncomfortable or awkward to speak up. As I begin to believe my voice matters to God, I am also learning that God gave me my unique voice to use boldly when my heart tells me something is just not right or a relationship is in need of healing. As our verse today reminds me, I am strengthened when I remember that I never face any battle alone.

We live in a world still broken by cruelty, inequality, and injustice. People can be unkind, and sometimes we treat each other unfairly. Resentments can grow and feelings can get hurt. Although withdrawal and cynicism may be appealing in the face of turmoil, nothing changes if we put our head in the sand and choose not to become part of the conversation.

Prayerfully and thoughtfully choosing to speak up in times of conflict is brave.

1. In what situation or relationship do you currently have the most difficulty speaking the truth in love?
2. Which is harder for you? Speaking your truth? Or speaking it with love?
3. What helps you to hear God's voice more clearly in times of conflict? How does knowing God is with you help you to be brave and speak up, even when it is uncomfortable?

Prayer: Lord, give us wisdom in communicating with the people in our lives. Help us know when it is better to remain silent and when we need to speak up. Show us how to speak the truth in love, always erring on the side of grace. God, help me be brave in the midst of conflict and discord, and give me a holy nudge when I am reluctant to rock a boat that needs to be rocked. Lord, give me the courage to speak up for those who have no voice and to be an advocate for those You love, including myself. Amen.

Day 6

A gentle answer will calm a person's anger,
but an unkind answer will cause more anger.

—*Proverbs 15:1 NCV*

Then Pilate said to Him, "Do You not hear all these things they are saying against You?" Jesus did not say a word. The leader was much surprised and wondered about it.

—*Matthew 27:13-14 NLV*

She was waiting for me when I returned to my car. I could see right away she was furious.

"You are so inconsiderate! You parked right in front of my mailbox! How dare you!"

My heart was pounding as I took a deep breath and considered my options. Perhaps a sarcastic comment about the wisdom of buying a house right across the street from a school? Or maybe I could just give her a dirty look, get in my car, and quickly drive away? How dare she lie in wait for me, then stand in the street screaming and shaking her finger at me?

However, since I had spent time in prayer earlier that morning, the Holy Spirit had followed me there and was whispering something else entirely.

She is hurting. Show her love. Show her grace.

A little disappointed to be robbed of my opportunity for a witty comeback or a dramatic stand, I decided to take the high road. I looked her in the eye and listened quietly until she ran out of words.

"I'm so sorry," I said. "You are right. I shouldn't have parked there. This must be so frustrating for you. I'm really very sorry."

She paused and then, not knowing how to deal with my response, she turned on her heel and stomped back into her house.

As I got back in my car, I was still shaking with emotion. The intensity of her anger made me feel vulnerable, and I was still struggling with the desire to lash out at her in return. In the past, I would have felt justified in returning fire for fire, unloading on her in retaliation. On this occasion, proximity to the Spirit led me to choose differently.

I wish I could say I always choose grace.

Several years later, I had the opportunity to learn more about the woman I met that day when she signed up for a Bible study I was leading in our community. She called after the first meeting to apologize for her long-ago outburst. She explained she had been intrigued by my kindness that day, so different from her expectations. Her curiosity ultimately led her to sign up for our study to find out more.

My decision to choose grace instead of anger that day ultimately made space for a new friend at the Kingdom table.

Being bold sometimes requires giving up our need to be right and choosing instead to be kind. While Jesus sometimes chose to confront the hypocrisy of the religious elite directly, in many other cases He simply listened, responded with questions, or remained silent altogether. In today's Scripture, even under the relentless questioning of Pontius Pilate in the final hours before His death, Jesus felt no need to defend

Himself because He knew who He was and to whom He belonged. His connection to His Father above gave Him strength to hold onto His convictions and not engage with those who would derail Him from His purpose.

Our Savior offers us the brave example of the power and strength sometimes found in silence.

1. Have you had an incident recently when you were faced with the choice to speak up or remain silent?
2. What difference does prayer make in your ability to choose your words wisely?
3. What is the hardest part about knowing when to take a stand and when to stand down?

Prayer: Gracious Father, help us choose our words wisely, particularly when emotions run high. Remind us to listen for the voice of the Holy Spirit in moments when we feel under attack. Only with Your help will we know whether to speak up boldly or choose a gentler path. Thank You for the example of Jesus who shows us that strength can often be found in silence. When we are faced with the choice of being right or being kind, help us choose wisely, strengthened by the power of Your spirit in us. You are so good, Father. Amen.

Being Brave
Is Being Resilient

Day 7

Be joyful in hope, patient in affliction, faithful in prayer.

—Romans 12:12

That person is like a tree planted by streams of water,
which yields its fruit in season
and whose leaf does not wither—
whatever they do prospers.

—Psalm 1:3

Being brave is being resilient.

Resilient people are both tough and flexible, steadfast and adept at changing.

There are two contrasting aspects to the definition of *resilience.*

- Stamina, endurance, toughness, and staying power
- Flexibility, adaptability, elasticity, and the ability to bounce back

Like a tree swaying in the wind, resilience allows us to stand firmly rooted in place yet bend without breaking as we face the storms of life.

My brave friend Jenny comes to mind when I think of the word *resilience.* Jenny has been battling a chronic, potentially life-threatening illness. Adjusting to her new normal, she told me recently she is learning to "embrace Plan B." The challenges she experiences are not her choice or preference. The ways in which her illness affects her life and the lives of her family are not part of her plans for this season of their life, and she would prefer for it to be different. Yet, as a person of faith, she trusts God will bring redemption and even joy through this journey. In the midst of her suffering, she actively engages in finding ways to participate in that process of redemption and looks for ways to encourage others who might be fighting similar battles. I am astonished by how often she finds reason to smile even in the midst of understandable despair. Like the tree in the storm, she relies on and nourishes the deep roots of her faith, while also adapting and changing as the situation requires. She stands firm and resolute, while simultaneously allowing the wind to invite her to a new and unexpected dance.

Hope is the antidote to despair when life gets hard. We cling to hope when we feel like giving up.

- We hope the latest medicine will finally work.
- We hope she will find someone to sit with at lunch.
- We hope the new job will come through.
- We hope he will return home soon.
- We hope she will stop drinking.
- We hope for the willpower to follow through on our goal.
- We hope this month there will be enough money to cover all the bills.
- We hope for healing. And forgiveness. And grace.

Because we believe someone who cares is listening to our prayers, we dare to hope for a change, an answer, a solution, a miracle.

While we are waiting for the answer to our prayer, we work hard to do our part and we look for evidence of joy. We lean into the encouragement of friends. We notice God's whispers in the beauty of a sunny day or a silent snow. We celebrate glimmers of progress and applaud baby steps of change. We laugh every time we get the chance because the world is as hilarious as it is painful. We pour out our hearts and allow our trusted friends to help us carry the weight of our sadness, fear, and anger when the burden becomes too heavy. We do the difficult work of counting our blessings, even when we must dig through our piles of worries to find them. We surround ourselves with prayer warriors to hold up our tired arms in the battle. We ask forgiveness when we mess up and we start again. We obey even when we are scared. We remember God's faithfulness and believe He is still right here with us in the midst of the mess, transforming every moment of suffering into the treasured gold forged only in the fire.

Choosing hope over despair is hard and holy work. Choosing to smile in the midst of our pain is an outward expression of our belief God is still in charge, still pursuing us, and still at work on our behalf. Choosing laughter alongside our tears is an offering and a sacrament to the grace and mercy of a good God who loves us and wants to heal our hurt.

In the storms of life, we cling to the knowledge of God's relentless love for us. Today, we choose hope. Today, we choose patience. And today, tomorrow, and the next, we choose to pray.

Being resilient is part of being brave.

1. In what areas of your life have you had to practice resilience?
2. Which aspect of resilience is more difficult for you? Endurance or flexibility?
3. Who in your life do you think of when you hear the word *resilience*? What do you admire most about them? Consider telling them how much you appreciate their example of courage in your life.

Prayer: Father, help us seek joy in the midst of sadness, laughter in the midst of tears, hope in the midst of despair. Give us the courage to count our blessings, even when they are buried under our worries. Remind us You are as close as our next breath and You love us more than we can ever comprehend. Build resilience in us so that we can be both strong and flexible as we face the storms of life. Surround us with people who are willing to enter with us into the dance. Amen.

Day 8

Consider it pure joy, my brothers, when you are involved in various trials, because you know that the testing of your faith produces endurance. But you must let endurance have its full effect, so that you may be mature and complete, lacking nothing.

—James 1:2-4 ISV

I am the vine; you are the branches. If you remain in me and I in you, you will bear much fruit; apart from me you can do nothing.

—John 15:5

Last year, I had the opportunity to join my husband on a business trip to Napa, California. Napa Valley is known as the wine country of California: the home of hundreds of miles of gently rolling hills, uniquely beautiful architecture, and acres and acres of breathtaking vineyards. Having a husband in the restaurant business clearly has its perks!

On our first day in Napa, my husband and I accompanied one other couple to their favorite winery, where we began our wine-tasting adventure. Our hostess seated us in comfy chairs with a heavenly view of the vineyards and taught us all about the process by which grapes become wine. She showed us samples of the dirt from their different vineyards and explained how the type of soil informs the distinct personalities of the different wines we were tasting. At one point in our conversation, in discussing irrigation processes in rocky soils, she said these words: "We want the vines to struggle. Vines that struggle produce better fruit."

She went on to explain that when the vines struggle to get water and nutrients from the soil, they form stronger, deeper roots. These stronger, deeper roots bring forth fruit that is richer, fuller, bigger, and juicier. Simply put, the struggle creates fruit that makes better wine. In grape growing and wine making, struggling is encouraged, promoted, and celebrated.

Does anyone else find it a relief to know that struggling vines produce better fruit?

Most of us are intimately acquainted with the concept of struggling, but what does struggling look like in our lives? Perhaps it includes the following from a dictionary definition of struggle: "fight, wrestle, grapple, strive, endeavor, compete, contend, scramble, flounder, stumble"—just a few of the synonyms for struggle. Several of these words, particularly the last few, feel familiar to me.

Sometimes our struggles are the result of circumstances outside our control. Job loss, health concerns, family drama, or issues in our larger society contribute to life feeling like more of a struggle than usual. Other times the struggle is more internal; the grappling, floundering, and wrestling found within the confines of my own mind. In these situations, when I compare my insides with other people's outsides, life seems easier for them. Others appear to be taking a more direct path to achieving their goals, instead of repeatedly getting in their own way like I often do.

But what if the struggling, the wrestling, the stumbling, the wandering is all part of the journey? What if the learning and growth happen *through* the struggling and not *in spite of* the struggling? What if, as part of that process, we learned to struggle well? To struggle wisely? What choices do we make during difficult times that make our struggle ultimately worth the cost?

Our Scripture verses today speak to this character-building aspect of dealing with questions, setbacks, and disappointments. Joy in the midst of trials requires intentional connection to something larger than ourselves, something or someone who can see the larger picture when we cannot. When we are in the midst of a crisis or challenge, it is difficult to believe a greater good is under construction and our struggle will be worth the pain. However, as we grow older, most of us begin to understand the gifts we receive in times of testing and failure. We discover we have in fact survived something we didn't believe we could endure, and we begin to trust in our own resilience and the faithfulness of God. We get back up, plant our feet firmly, and take a step forward into the next right thing. We adjust to changes we never thought we would have to make and learn we are capable of learning new ways of being—a work in progress, a masterpiece in the making. On the other side, we see the ways in which God used our friends, family, and circumstances to lift us up and carry us through, and we begin to discover the depth of our strength. Connected to our Source, we are survivors and we learn to call ourselves brave.

For us and for grapevines, struggling is part of the process. For us and for grapevines, deeper and stronger roots connect us to the source of that which gives us life. For us and for grapevines, it is God who ultimately brings whatever fruit we bear.

1. Do you believe learning comes from struggling? What is an example of this from your own life?
2. In recent months, has your struggling been mostly external or internal?
3. What does struggling well look like for you? What do today's Scriptures have to offer you about choosing to struggle well?

Prayer: Father, You are the Source of all we need to live lives of meaning and purpose. Help us remain in Your love and stay connected to You through prayer and time in Your word. Remind us when we struggle that struggling is part of the process and helps us grow. We want deeper roots, so that we can bear richer, fuller, life-giving fruit. You tell us the fruit of Your spirit is love, joy, peace, patience, kindness, goodness, faithfulness, gentleness, and self-control. We trust You to produce this kind of fruit in us as we abide in You. Amen.

Day 9

But we have this treasure in jars of clay to show that this all-surpassing power is from God and not from us. We are hard pressed on every side, but not crushed; perplexed, but not in despair; persecuted, but not abandoned; struck down, but not destroyed.

—2 Corinthians 4:7-9

Let us hold unswervingly to the hope we profess, for he who promised is faithful.

—Hebrews 10:23

My friend Linda is a brave warrior. Diagnosed with breast cancer, she faced chemotherapy, major surgery, and radiation. She gathered her troops and laid out the battle plan. We formed our battle strategy on a stormy fall day as we waded through the muddy swollen creek near her house. Our destination was her favorite prayer rock, where we joined hands and poured out our broken hearts to our listening Father. As we stood praying in the rain, it was difficult to determine the source of the moisture on each of our cheeks. We were scared but ready to do whatever was necessary to see our beloved sister through this challenge.

Cancer is not for cowards, and the next year was difficult. Along with the daunting physical challenges, she and her family had to adjust to the necessity of asking for help. As her husband and three kids attempted to fill in for their mom, her friends showed up with food, cleaning supplies, and stacks of DVDs. Some days we also provided much-needed laughter and conversation. Other days, when she was too sick to lift her head, we told her how brave she was, refilled her water bottle, kissed her on the cheek, and threw in one more load of laundry on our way out the door. During the hardest days, Linda dug deep in her reservoir of courage and kept her eye on the finish line. As she completed each milestone of treatment—chemotherapy then surgery then radiation—we celebrated and prayed for the day she would be looking at this battle in her rearview mirror.

Like all cancer survivors, Linda has been changed by her experience. Now cancer-free, she knows she can do hard things and emerge all the stronger. She knows that she is brave and that God is faithful. She often serves as a resource to others facing a cancer diagnosis and those who love them. She knows firsthand the depth of faith forged in the fire. While painful and frightening, her journey with cancer ultimately made her stronger, and that strength has been translated into a new career path and opportunities to serve others. Like many others in her situation, her priorities are clearer, and she is no longer willing to waste time on nonsense. As He so often does, God has used her difficult experience to create something beautiful out of the ashes.

When we are facing uncertain circumstances, our strength and courage are uncovered little by little. Resilience is showing up and doing the next right thing, taking the next baby step forward, one moment at a time. The next right thing is discovered by leaning in and listening carefully to the voice of God. Sometimes that voice sounds like reassurance deep in our spirit as we search for strength. Other times it sounds more like the gentle reprimand of a friend telling us to get back in bed, get some rest, and try again tomorrow.

1. Can you think of a circumstance in life in which you felt "struck down but not destroyed"?
2. How did you find the courage to get through that circumstance?
3. How did the people in your life help you get through that circumstance? What did you find most helpful? What did people do that was *not* helpful?

Prayer: God, please give us a deeper experience of Your presence and strength in the midst of crisis. Thank You for the people You send to build us up in tough times, and give us the courage to accept the help they offer. Show us how to love each other well, even when it feels awkward. During times of difficulty, open our eyes to the moments of beauty we might otherwise miss. We trust You to give us everything we need to walk through the fire and hear Your voice showing us the next right thing. Amen.

Day 10

Don't worry about anything; instead, pray about everything. Tell God what you need, and thank him for all he has done. Then you will experience God's peace, which exceeds anything we can understand. His peace will guard your hearts and minds as you live in Christ Jesus.

—Philippians 4:6-7 NLT

Don't copy the behavior and customs of this world, but let God transform you into a new person by changing the way you think. Then you will learn to know God's will for you, which is good and pleasing and perfect.

—Romans 12:2 NLT

As the beginning of sixth grade approached, my daughter Brooke became overwhelmed by worry. She would lay awake at night, tossing and turning, until she would finally come downstairs in tears. "I can't sleep. I will *never* fall asleep!"

Each night, my husband or I would walk her back up to bed and try to talk through the concerns weighing so heavily on her mind. Although we tried to assuage her fears and reassure her about her ability to handle each of the scenarios she presented, the process of listing her worries only served to heighten her anxiety. It was clear we needed a new plan to deal with this escalating situation.

As I prayed about how to help my daughter, I remembered today's first verse. I typed out Philippians 4:6-7 in two different translations and, when bedtime approached, we tried something new.

Instead of rehearsing her fears and worries, we asked her instead to remember all the good things going on in her life that day. We read through the verse together and then we prayed for peace and a good night's sleep. We left the verse next to her bed and encouraged her to read it again if she started to feel overwhelmed by her worries. The transition wasn't immediate, but over the course of the next week or so, she began to feel calmer about the coming school year and her nocturnal visits for reassurance lessened. Throughout her adolescence, she returned to this verse again and again in times of trouble.

Gratitude and prayer. The prescription for peace? The secret of resilience? A quick fix to make our worries instantly disappear?

Or a practical, intentional way to refocus our mind and reconnect with the God in whose image we are made?

Changing our feelings and behavior often starts with changing our mind. Our thoughts hold great power, and allowing God to change the way we think can be the beginning of healing. Replacing self-defeating thoughts with the truth of who we are in Christ may take time, but it is worth the effort. While counting our blessings might seem to be the stuff of children's lullabies, developing a habit of gratitude is actually a practical way to partner with God in the process of transforming our thoughts and, ultimately, the way we feel.

Life is often messy and hard. We can become overwhelmed by the weight of our worries, both real and perceived. Our fears paralyze us and hold us back in a place where our dreams are just out of reach. We want to move forward, but we repeatedly find ourselves stuck. To do battle with those voices restraining us and keeping us up at night, a shift in perspective is necessary. Centering ourselves in the presence of God and remembering the ways we have already seen His hand at work in our lives reminds us we are not alone. As we make prayer and gratitude a habit, we find we have the strength and courage to move forward and try again.

1. What fear most frequently keeps you up at night?
2. What lies do the voices of fear, doubt, and worry tell you? How do you know they are lies?
3. Have you ever engaged in a gratitude practice such as writing down three things for which you are thankful at the end of the day? If so, what did you find helpful in being intentional about thankfulness?

Prayer: Strong Father, remind us You are bigger than our fears. Help us remember Your perfect peace is available to us, if only we come to You. Make us aware of the self-defeating thoughts to which we regularly give power and help us to find words of truth from Scripture to change those thoughts. Remind us of the wisdom of regularly giving thanks and help us to develop an attitude of gratitude. Give us the wisdom to learn healthy ways of dealing with our worries and remind us we are brave. Speak loudly, Father, so loudly You drown out the unwelcome voices of worry and fear. Amen.

Day 11

Therefore, since we are surrounded by such a great cloud of witnesses, let us throw off everything that hinders and the sin that so easily entangles. And let us run with perseverance the race marked out for us, fixing our eyes on Jesus, the pioneer and perfecter of faith.

—Hebrews 12:1-2

I'm not saying that I have this all together, that I have it made. But I am well on my way, reaching out for Christ, who has so wondrously reached out for me. Friends, don't get me wrong: By no means do I count myself an expert in all of this, but I've got my eye on the goal, where God is beckoning us onward—to Jesus. I'm off and running, and I'm not turning back.

—Philippians 3:12-14 MSG

One beautiful May day several years ago, as I headed down to our basement to work out, I found myself wishing that my exercise routine could be done outside instead. The flowers were blooming, the trees were budding, and the temperature was a perfect seventy-five degrees. The obvious choice would be to go for a run, but I was convinced running was not for me. My sister is a runner. My brother is a runner. Kelly is not a runner. I had tried before to run and couldn't do it. I hated running. I was bad at it. I wasn't built to run, and I had made my mind up about it.

However, that May, the idea of exercising outside persisted. I went online to look up walking programs, thinking that perhaps a fast walk on a pretty day would be a nice addition to my exercise repertoire. Long story short, I ran across an app for my iPhone that promised a gradual progression from walker to runner. I took a chance and gave it a try, and over the course of several months, I became a runner.

Running is a process. And running "the race set before us" is a process as well. Both endeavors take consistency, practice, and perseverance. It doesn't happen overnight, and, when I fail, I must start over and begin again. I keep trying, and I persevere, even when I don't see immediate results, because I am beginning to trust that the process itself is valuable. The time I invest in trying new things and building healthier habits, whether physical or spiritual, is never wasted. I am in charge of participating in the process; God is in charge of the results. I show up and do the work and leave the rest to God.

In our walk with God, we often don't see our progress until we are looking in the rearview mirror. For centuries, the people of God have practiced the spiritual disciplines of our faith, trusting God will meet us there. We show up in the silence through confession, prayer, Scripture reading, and meditation. We show up in celebration through worship, fellowship, and service to others. We participate in the sacraments of baptism and communion, believing that our proximity to God will change us, heal us, and transform us. We know these practices do not earn us God's love, but we trust they are gifts of God's grace. God loves us too much to allow us to settle for anything less than the fullest expression of who He created us to be. Obedience is our path to peace and spiritual maturity.

I ran a 5K race a couple of years after I started running. I didn't break any records, but I finished in a respectable amount of time. I loved the process of participating side by side with the other runners and being encouraged across the finish line by the cheering spectators. It is that scene I picture when I read today's verse. Arriving at the finish line the morning of the race may have seemed like it happened in a little over thirty minutes. In reality, it took much, much longer. It involved me getting over the idea that I would never be a runner. It required me listening to people who knew more about learning to run than I did and following their advice. It required me spending many months alternating between walking and running before I could finally run the whole way. It took me putting on my workout clothes and running shoes every Monday, Wednesday, and Friday, whether I felt like it or not. But ultimately, the process and perseverance paid off. Now, to my delighted surprise, I am a runner!

1. What does the word *perseverance* mean to you? In what area of your life have you been able to persevere? In what area of your life is persevering particularly difficult?
2. What stories have you told yourself about your ability to be successful in pursuing a goal that is important to you? How might you rewrite that story to achieve different results?
3. Both of our Scriptures today talk about keeping our eye on the goal. What does it mean for you to keep your eye on the goal in your life right now? How would you define your primary goal?

Prayer: Patient Father, help us be people who persevere. Teach us to be patient with ourselves as we slowly build the kinds of habits that contribute to our being our better selves. Give us the courage to try something new and the grace to start again when we get sidetracked or discouraged. We know we are people capable of learning and growing. Remind us of that fact when we forget. Remind us of the cloud of witnesses cheering us on and help us keep our eye on the goal. Amen.

Day 12

And let us not grow weary of doing good, for in due season we will reap, if we do not give up.

—Galatians 6:9 ESV

I planted the seed, Apollos watered it, but God has been making it grow. So neither the one who plants nor the one who waters is anything, but only God, who makes things grow.

—1 Corinthians 3:6-7

I recently traveled to Europe and had the opportunity to take a tour of the breathtaking cathedral that towers over the ancient city of Milan, the Duomo di Milano. The Duomo is the fifth largest Christian church in the world and the second largest in Italy. Begun in 1386, construction took more than six centuries. I purchased the headset guide and listened to the story of the centuries of work it took to construct a structure of this magnitude. As I climbed the 250 steps to the roof, I thought about the lives of the people who labored for decades to create this magnificent work of art, most of them giving their lives to the project and never seeing its completion. On the roof, I found many examples of the intricately carved stone gargoyles painstakingly fashioned by artists centuries before my birth, now silently standing guard over a modern city their creators could never have imagined.

In our Internet world, it is hard to wait. We are accustomed to instant gratification, answers to every question accessible with a few keystrokes. We text a friend or family member and become frustrated when we don't get an immediate response. Buildings, which once took decades to build, seemingly appear overnight with the help of modern equipment and state-of-the-art technology. We can no longer imagine investing our lives in a project we would never see completed.

As a gardener, I love the imagery found in today's verses of planting seeds and waiting for the harvest. Gardening reminds me of the privilege of participating in the act of creating, the waiting time required for results, and the limitations of my personal power in the process. A passion for flowers and a willingness to get dirty is what I contribute to creating the beauty of my garden. The transformation of ugly dirt into colorful blooms is entirely God's job. No matter how hard I work, I can't create a single flower on my own. What I can do, however, is provide an environment in which God can work His magic. Providing fertile soil, planting flowers in the appropriate aspect, making sure the weeds don't get too thick and the plants don't go too long without water are my attempts at participating in the miracle of creation. And even as I do my part, I still must wait to see the results of my labor.

Similarly, much of what we are called to do as followers of Jesus does not yield immediate results. We invest in the lives of our families, our friends, and our communities, but the fruit of our labor is often hidden from our view. We pour ourselves out by loving and serving those whom God places in our path, and we hope, like the time I spend in my garden, our offerings will be transformed into something beautiful. We trust in a good God and the promises of the coming Kingdom, believing our participation matters. Each time we plant seeds of kindness, mercy, and grace, we believe it is the beginning of something God can use. Our labor is not wasted, even when we can't see the results.

Like the builders of the ancient cathedral, God has given each of us a part to play in the masterpiece He is creating, but only God can see the final product. Occasionally, our gracious God pulls back the curtain, and we see a glimpse of that which will be, and we know we are part of something bigger and more beautiful than we could ever have created on our own.

1. Where are the places in your life where you are planting seeds? Family, work, community?
2. In what ways have you been encouraged that the seeds you are planting are bearing or will bear fruit? In what ways have you been discouraged or fearful that your efforts are in vain?
3. How do today's verses help you build resilience and continue moving forward in pursuing your goal of being braver?

Prayer: God, remind us we are only responsible for the process. We show up and do the next right thing. We bring our passions, our talents, and our willingness to roll up our sleeves and get dirty. You bring about results in Your timing. Help us trust that the seeds of love and kindness we plant now will ultimately bear fruit. Make us brave enough to invest in that which we cannot see, knowing You see all. Amen.

Day 13

Then he returned to the disciples and found them asleep. He said to Peter, "Couldn't you watch with me even one hour? Keep watch and pray, so that you will not give in to temptation. For the spirit is willing, but the body is weak!"

—Matthew 26:40-41 NLT

A third time he asked him, "Simon son of John, do you love me?" Peter was hurt that Jesus asked the question a third time. He said, "Lord, you know everything. You know that I love you." Jesus said, "Then feed my sheep."

—John 21:17 NLT

Peter is one of my favorite people in the Bible. In fact, I am completely crazy about Peter.

Peter was part of Jesus's inner circle, one of the three disciples who often accompanied Jesus into the more intimate moments of His ministry. On the night of His arrest, Jesus asks Peter, John, and James to follow Him farther into the Garden of Gethsemane, where He shares with them the extent of His distress and asks them to watch and pray with Him. Although they love Jesus, they struggle to stay alert. Startled awake when the soldiers arrive to arrest Jesus, Peter cuts off the ear of one of the soldiers in a brave but foolhardy attempt to protect his master. Later that same night, his courage waning, Peter runs in the opposite direction and repeatedly denies knowing Jesus.

In Scripture, Peter is painted as a man of passion, complicated and real. He wants to be close to Jesus, yet he often finds himself jumping in over his head in his enthusiasm. Peter was Jesus's right-hand man: a natural leader, energetic, confident, and ready for anything. From the moment Jesus calls Peter to follow Him, He sees Peter's potential and tells him he is the rock on which God will build the church. Despite His faith in Peter, Jesus frequently challenges and corrects Peter to temper his rough edges and mold him into the leader Jesus knows he will someday be. Again and again, Jesus says to Peter, "Watch me. Listen to me. Follow me."

Peter, like all of us, is a work in progress. He gives up everything to follow Jesus and then fails spectacularly in the heat of the moment, just as Jesus predicted he would. Yet, despite Peter's betrayal, Jesus continues to see him as the person God the Father created him to be. In today's second verse, after feeding him breakfast, Jesus reminds Peter who he is, who he loves, and to whom he belongs. Three times, Jesus asks Peter the question, "Do you love me?" Three times, with increasing fervor, Peter says, "Yes, Lord, you know I love you!" And with each declaration of love, Jesus offers forgiveness and beckons Peter forward into his calling with the entreaty, "Feed my sheep."

Part of being brave is getting back up when we fall down. Like Peter, we are messy: full of contradictions and mixed motives. We want to be faithful and fearless, but our worries and weaknesses often get in the way. We try, we mess up, and we try again. Resilience and tenacity are often forged in the fires of our failures. When we know we are fully loved in spite of our wandering ways, we can be confident as we seek forgiveness and begin again. Like Peter, God never gives up on us, continually working in our lives to transform us into our braver, better, bolder selves. Being brave does not mean we are perfect; being brave means accepting Jesus's gift of forgiveness and trying again.

1. Name one critical failure you have experienced, what led to that failure, and what you learned from it.
2. Who is one of your favorite characters in the Bible and how does that character's story encourage you to be brave and keep trying?
3. If you are not familiar with the disciple Peter, here are a few other places in Scripture where you can read more about his story: Luke 5:1-11, Matthew 14:22-33, Mark 9:2-10, Acts 2:14-47. What do you like best about Peter?

Prayer: Faithful Father, thank You for never giving up on us. What a blessing it is to know that no matter how many times we fail, You are there to welcome us back with arms open wide in love and forgiveness. When we fall, encourage us to get back up and try again with Your help. Through the power of the Holy Spirit in our lives, we know You are working in our lives to transform us into the person You know we can be. Like Peter, we know the path forward lies in our deep and abiding love for You. Amen.

PART 2

Love

For God has not given us a spirit of fear and timidity, but of power, LOVE, and self-discipline.

—2 Timothy 1:7 NLT

We *love* because God first loved us. Jesus reminds us the most important commandment is to love God with all our heart and to love one another as we love ourselves. Our theme verse tells us God has given each of us a spirit of love, yet many of us feel disconnected and lonely. Although God has created us for community, we often hide from one another in our more tender places. Comparison, competition, and perfectionism block connection and keep us stuck believing we are irreparably separated. Authenticity and vulnerability break down those walls and build the connection we long for, the connection for which we were made. Listening to one another and naming one another brave is the path back to God and to the bigger, braver life we desire. In this section, we will explore what it means to be *authentic* and *vulnerable,* deepening our connections to one another and experiencing the depth of God's spirit of love.

Being Brave
Is Being Authentic

Day 14

Taste and see that the Lord is good;
blessed is the one who takes refuge in him.

—*Psalm 34:8*

Surely your goodness and unfailing love will pursue me
all the days of my life,
and I will live in the house of the Lord
forever.

—*Psalm 23:6 NLT*

Being brave is being authentic.

Jesus and I have been friends for a long time. Even as a child, I believed my prayers were heard and God was on my side. I talked to God regularly; however, I sometimes felt as if I didn't fit in at church. I never doubted God's love and presence, but I didn't always feel particularly proficient at being a church kid. I wanted to be a good Christian, but I didn't know if I could ever be like the "good Christians" I thought I was supposed to emulate.

As a teenager, I was confused. I committed myself to God over and over again, thinking that I hadn't quite gotten it right because I still wasn't like "them." I wanted to be a "good Christian," but some of the religious people to whom I was looking for guidance had ideas that didn't feel right to me. I acted one way with my church friends and another way with my other friends, trying to be who I thought everyone wanted me to be. I only succeeded in feeling guilty about the ways I could never measure up to what I believed was expected of me by both groups. In many ways, I was too wild and free-spirited to fit in with the "religious" kids and yet too crazy about Jesus to feel at home with the wild kids. Like many adolescents, I didn't know which one was the "real" me.

As I got older, and life seemed more complicated, it often felt as if I were chasing God—trying to please Him, get His attention, earn His love and favor. As I understood the ways of the world better, grace made less and less sense. Being a "good" Christian seemed to require work and the following of formulas—a process at which I never felt terribly successful. Being a person that is skeptical of authority and prone to in-depth analysis, I questioned and fought and studied my way to a shaky obedience and a lukewarm truce with religion as I understood it.

Then, in my early thirties, I fell in love with the Bible. Through a series of divinely ordained coincidences, I found myself involved in a series of Bible studies written for women, in which we were encouraged to "taste and see." Surrounded by other women and hungry for a deeper experience of God, I dug in, "tasted," and found something very good indeed. Through a deeper appreciation and exploration of God's word as revealed in the Bible, I also fell in love with God in a whole new way.

Here is what I heard that changed my life: every time I ever thought of God, it was because He thought of me first. Even though I believed I was chasing God, it was actually God who was chasing me. Being part of my life was always God's idea. The Bible was the story of God seeking to draw His people closer, and, like the people in those stories, God's fingerprints were all over my story, my life, my journey. God had been there all along inviting me into the story He was telling and the work He was doing. He was crazy about me and would stop at nothing to woo me, love me, cherish me, and pour His Spirit into me. God never intended for me to change the way He made me in order to become some sanitized version of myself that appeared holier and more proper. I was simply called to love God with all my heart, soul, mind, and spirit, and to love others as myself by being the uniquely gifted person God made me to be. God would take care of any needed transformation as I leaned on Him. God's Spirit of strength, peace, and power was available to me every moment, not because I had earned it but as a gift from One who loved me completely.

This realization changed everything. I quit chasing God and allowed God to "catch" me. This distinction has made all the difference.

Here is what I know to be true: if you are reading these words, God is chasing you too. God already loves you completely exactly as you are. God is not waiting for you to be a better, holier version of yourself to love you and use you in His kingdom plan. You don't have to pretend to be someone you are not in order to be on God's team. God says, "Come as you are." God's plan to love, heal, and redeem His kingdom will not be complete without you, the real you, the you God made and loves. Being our authentic selves, in relationship with our good God, is the path to a life of freedom, meaning, and adventure.

Being authentic is part of being brave.

1. Who introduced you to the idea of prayer? Did you pray as a child?

2. What is your understanding of the difference between a relationship with God and the practice of religion?
3. How does it change things for you if you believe God is pursuing you, instead of you pursuing Him?

Prayer: Relentless and pursuing God, what an amazing realization it is when we get a glimpse of Your love for us! You created us to be in relationship with You, and You will never give up pursuing us. Remind us we are safe in Your love, so we can quit running. Help us stop, turn back to You, and allow You to finally catch us and make us Your own. You are so good and love us just as we are in this moment. Thank You for never giving up on us! Amen.

Day 15

For we are God's handiwork, created in Christ Jesus to do good works, which God prepared in advance for us to do.

—Ephesians 2:10

For God did not send his Son into the world to condemn the world, but to save the world through him.

—John 3:17

"I'm so stupid! I can't do anything right. I'll never be able to do this! I'm an idiot." Frustrated and overwhelmed, my daughter threw up her hands in despair and plopped her head down face first onto the kitchen table in defeat. I wasn't sure either one of us was going to survive another round with her math homework. A strong writer and an imaginative storyteller, she saw numbers as her nemesis. Despite her good grades in other subjects, she considered her increasing struggle with math as irrefutable evidence of her lack of intelligence. Math was hard, so clearly she was stupid.

"Stop calling my little girl stupid."

When she heard my stern voice, she raised her head out of her dramatic slump and looked at me quizzically. I repeated myself.

"I mean it. Stop calling my daughter names. Stop calling my little girl stupid. She is not stupid, and I don't like you calling her names."

She smiled at my silliness as she realized I was referring to her, my little girl. I looked at her and once again reiterated my admonition about her self-reproach.

"You, my love, are not stupid. Some things are easy for you. Other things are more difficult, so you will have to work harder. But you can do hard things."

Although not quite as dramatic as my daughter, I often fall into the same trap of beating myself up, quick to list all the ways I fall short. No one is more intimately familiar with the places I don't measure up, the areas where I am not enough. I imagine our heavenly Father offering a similar response when we call ourselves names and berate ourselves for our failures. We are tough on ourselves, and our inner critic can be so mean.

"Failure, fat, stupid, lazy, ugly! You will never get it right; you always mess up. What makes you think you can do it this time?"

God says otherwise.

Recognizing and refusing to cooperate with the voice of our inner critic is part of how we partner with God in the work He is doing in our lives. Our inner critic is a saboteur and speaks the language of shame and lies. Although it is important to acknowledge both our strengths and our weaknesses, God never intends for us to drown in shame and condemnation. Filling our minds with the truth of God's word allows us to turn up the volume on God's voice and turn down the volume on the one who would keep us feeling defeated, scared, and stuck.

In order to be brave, we must repeatedly choose who we allow to name us.

God says His children are redeemed, holy, forgiven, empowered by the Holy Spirit, brave, and beloved. God created us and uniquely equipped each of us with gifts, talents, strengths, proclivities, and passions that He intends for us to use for the benefit of our hurting and broken world. When we give in to despair and defeat, we are denying our birthright and our powerful identity as children of God. Yes, we are a work in progress, but we are the handiwork of the Creator of the universe. We are in good hands. The masterpiece is not yet complete.

Friend, stop calling God's beloved daughter names. Some things will be easy for you. Some things will be harder, but you can do hard things. You are the daughter of the King.

1. What names does your inner critic call you?
2. What things are easy for you? What things are harder?
3. How do you determine the difference between God's voice of loving conviction and the unhealthy voice of condemnation and shame?

Prayer: Father, next time the voice of my inner critic gets too loud, remind me that she speaks the language of lies. You are the author of truth and You call me Beloved. While You may sometimes speak words of loving conviction when we have wandered away from You, You never speak words of condemnation. Help us acknowledge the places we fall short, ask for forgiveness, and submit to Your transforming work in our lives. We choose to listen to Your voice, Lord, so turn up the volume! Amen.

Day 16

For you created my inmost being;
you knit me together in my mother's womb.
I praise you because I am fearfully and wonderfully made;
your works are wonderful,
I know that full well.

—*Psalm 139:13-14*

For just as each of us has one body with many members, and these members do not all have the same function, so in Christ we, though many, form one body, and each member belongs to all the others. We have different gifts, according to the grace given to each of us.

—*Romans 12:4-6*

My friend Linda vacationed at a dude ranch in Montana. She went by herself because her husband did not choose to spend his vacation with cattle. He held down the fort at home with their three kids and sent her, with his blessing, for her fortieth birthday celebration. She camped out a few of the nights, and one morning woke up to the refreshing temperature of twenty-two degrees. She shared her lodging for part of the time with something actually called a pack rat. But her favorite thing—the activity she particularly enjoyed—was cow pinning. If you knew Linda, you would enjoy this picture, as she is about five feet tall and probably doesn't weigh ninety-five pounds. *Cow* pinning! I had to ask her to repeat the exact phrase several times. My tiny friend Linda went to Montana on a vacation by herself, slept with rats, rode horses, pinned cows, and had the time of her life.

Truthfully, I was a little jealous.

Let me be quite clear that I am not one bit jealous of the actual vacation. In my wildest dreams, I have never wanted to chase a cow or sleep in a tent when it is twenty-two degrees. However, I have wanted to be the kind of girl who *wanted* to do adventurous things like that—parachute, climb mountains, bike through the Himalayas, sleep in the wilderness. In theory, I like the idea of *wanting* to go to Montana and pin cows. I think she is amazingly brave for following through on her dream and doing it.

I have also wanted to be the type of person who plays sports and enjoys exercise. Instead, I exercise only because I want to be able to garden when I am old and because I hate it when my pants are too tight. As a matter of fact, gardening is about as adventurous and outdoorsy as I get, and only because I get the payoff of beautiful flowers at the end.

So even though I might want to be an athletic, adventurous, sailboat-sailing, mountain-biking, dig-my-own-latrine, cow-pinning gal, it is just not who I am. I am someone quite different. For whatever reason, God made me like this. Even though I am uncoordinated and consistently trip over my own feet, God gave me other gifts, talents, and interests. I won't ever be picked for the church softball team, but they enjoy having me in the choir. I would never jump out of an airplane, but I don't mind performing on a stage to a full house. The more time I spend wishing I was more like *[fill in the blank]*, the less time I have for figuring out why God made me the way He did. Apparently, God has a plan for a person just like me, right now, in this place. To be clear, it certainly doesn't hurt us to try new things and step outside of our comfort zone at times. But when we waste our time trying to mold ourselves into being a certain type of person we think we *ought* to be, someone whom we weren't ever *meant* to be, we miss out on the opportunity to let God show us why He made us who we are.

1. Is there some personality trait you wish you had but don't?
2. What is one thing you do well? What is one thing you particularly like about yourself?
3. How does comparison with others get in the way of you being brave?

Prayer: Creator God, thank You for making so many different versions of Your children. You have put so many interesting and inspiring people in my life, but I sometimes get distracted by comparing myself to them. The next time I start to wish I were more like someone else, whisper in my ear and remind me You made me in a very particular way. The world is better for having me in it because You don't make mistakes. You made me and I am Your beloved, just the way I am. Amen.

Day 17

He brought me out into a spacious place;
he rescued me because he delighted in me.

—*2 Samuel 22:20*

You have not given me into the hands of the enemy
but have set my feet in a spacious place.

—*Psalm 31:8*

After fifty-two years of research on the subject, and a firm grasp of the obvious, it appears I will not be able to achieve anything close to perfection in this lifetime. Perhaps perfection isn't exactly the word, but the more I think about the things that keep me stuck, the more I realize I have secretly harbored an unrealistic vision of what being a grown-up looks like. I think I expected a certain completeness, a sense of having arrived at the final version of me. I had hoped by now to have achieved a clarity of calling, the right balance of work and play, healthy relationships with food, my body, my family, my friends, my money, my colleagues, the church, and God. Check, check, check. All done! I have arrived! Yay Team!

The trouble begins when I interpret anything less than this utopian ideal to be failure.

When I set a vision of perfection or being "complete" as the goal, the inevitable mistakes and detours of life become the enemy and repeated failure the result. My failure defines me and I am never, ever enough. When I operate from this belief—when I believe I am a failure and not enough—I am always struggling to prove my worthiness. Perfection is a moving target, and constantly hustling for worthiness and striving toward some nebulous definition of "good" makes me feel as if I'm trapped on a hamster wheel. Stuck, going nowhere in a hurry.

In today's verses, God mentions a place of rescue, refuge, and rest, which He calls "a spacious place." I am coming to understand that this spacious place to which we are invited is:

- a place of learning, growing, exploring, forgiveness, redemption, and joy
- a place where we are free to try new things, make mistakes, and learn from them
- a place free from the tyranny of self-absorption and eternal navel-gazing
- a way out of the comparison and competition game
- a place where our only measure of success is moving ever closer to the heart of God and His kingdom

A spacious place is the opposite of boxed in, backed into a corner, and not being able to find a way out of places. A spacious place is full of opportunity and possibility. Don't miss the part in the verse from Psalm 18 in which we learn the reason for our invitation to the spacious place: God delights in us! God has named us "Beloved."

Simply put, God has invited us to come outside into the fresh air to play. God is wooing us from the jaws of expectation and perfection distress. God is inviting us to embrace progress, not perfection. God is inviting us to continue to struggle well, leaning on Him for the strength to get through the hard places and thanking Him when the road is smooth. My process of transformation, which God promises He will complete in His perfect timing, is better left in His capable hands. My job is to show up, be real, ask forgiveness when I fail, do the next right thing, and love God and His people with all my heart, mind, soul, and spirit.

1. What expectations keep you stuck? Do those expectations come from yourself or others?
2. What do you imagine your spacious place looks and feels like?
3. How do you feel about progress, not perfection, as a goal?

Prayer: Dear Father, take me by the hand and lead me to the spacious place You promise! Remind me my goal is progress, not perfection, and strengthen me as I lean on You in the process of becoming my best self. You have begun a good work in me, and You will bring it to completion in Your perfect time. Thank You for loving me so much and believing I am enough just like I am. Amen.

Day 18

Share each other's burdens, and in this way obey the law of Christ.

—Galatians 6:2 NLT

He walked away, perhaps a stone's throw, and knelt down and prayed this prayer: "Father, if you are willing, please take away this cup of horror from me. But I want your will, not mine." Then an angel from heaven appeared and strengthened him, for he was in such agony of spirit that he broke into a sweat of blood, with great drops falling to the ground as he prayed more and more earnestly.

—Luke 22:42-44 TLB

For years, we had a bowl on the kitchen counter for the accumulated clutter that had no other home. The bowl, which I referred to as the "scary bowl," was the receptacle for the items I was planning to put away later—the stuff I would find a place for in the faraway land of Someday. To be honest, in addition to the scary bowl, we also had a few scary drawers, but these were hidden from sight. The scary bowl was in full view, and, because of its convenient location, it was always full to overflowing with the debris and mess of our lives. It was, to put it mildly, a bit of an eyesore. When company was on the way over, the scary bowl was quickly moved to its other home on top of the washing machine, safely out of sight behind the closed door of the laundry room.

After all, what would people think if they saw the level of our clutter and disorganization?

My "scary bowl" is a great metaphor for the masks many of us wear. We all have those parts of ourselves that are not so pretty, the unflattering, can't-quite-get-it-all-together-for-company parts. We all have places of doubt, fear, insecurity, jealousy, and impatience. This part from within us says ugly things about our neighbors, yells at our family, or ignores someone who is hurting because we are just too busy. This is the part of me that compares myself to others who seem so much more in control of their lives and cause me to wonder what I am doing wrong. Or maybe this is the part of us that seems to consistently fall short despite our desire to do better. Maybe it is the part of me that has big questions for God when everyone else seems so certain or even the part that battles a secret habit or addiction all alone. All of this, all the emotional clutter that piles up in our lives for which we don't have a place or don't want to deal, makes up our big "scary bowl" of stuff that we choose to hide from others and from God with our smiling faces and occasional "Praise the Lord."

While it should be just the opposite, the church can sometimes be a place where we especially feel the need to hide our messiness, darkness, and fear. We reprimand ourselves that if we had more faith, we could rise above our worries and struggles. Or we tell ourselves that others seem to have figured out how to make it work, so we'd better not let on that it just isn't easy for us. We shine the light of our good side but keep the darker parts hidden from view. Because we associate sharing our tender places with weakness, we pretend to be tough and hide our vulnerable moments from each other and God.

Yet God never intended for us to hide out and get through life's tough times alone.

In today's verses, our completely perfect Savior shows us the strength found in allowing others to help us carry our burdens. On the night of His arrest, before the soldiers arrived, Jesus retreated to the Garden of Gethsemane to pray. Scripture tells us Jesus was overcome with despair and begged God to spare Him from the coming horror. Jesus poured out His heart to God, even as He obediently accepted His part in the Father's plan for our redemption. Jesus was in such agony of spirit, He sweat drops of blood as He prayed more and more earnestly. Yet during this long night, Jesus frequently checked in with the disciples standing watch with Him. Instead of pretending He was fearless, Jesus shared the depth of His heartbreak with His friends. As Jesus lamented their inability to stay awake, He told them He was overwhelmed with sorrow to the point of death. Even Jesus, fully God and fully man, honestly poured out His heart to God *and* His friends when He was filled with fear and doubt.

Sharing our fears and allowing someone else to help us carry the weight of our burdens are signs of courage and strength, not weakness. We are not created to carry our burdens and heartache alone. Sharing ourselves, our real selves, is part of being brave.

1. What parts of your life do you hide from others? What is your greatest fear about sharing those parts of yourself?
2. Who are the people who know about your "scary bowl"?
3. What advantages or benefits have you experienced in the past when you have shared your "messiness" with someone

else? What makes it easier to do so? How can you be that person for someone else?

Prayer: Lord, help me be brave enough to share my real self with others. Point me in the direction of those safe friends and family with whom I can truly be myself. When I am tempted to hide behind a happy, shiny mask of false cheerfulness or manufactured competence, remind me I am loved deeply even with my imperfections. Remind us that even Jesus, who was perfect in every way, was willing to share His heart with His friends and with His Father. Amen.

Day 19

So God created mankind in his own image,
in the image of God he created them;
male and female he created them.

—Genesis 1:27

He makes the whole body fit together perfectly. As each part does its own special work, it helps the other parts grow, so that the whole body is healthy and growing and full of love.

—Ephesians 4:16 NLT

"When I grow up, I want to be like Judy." I muttered these words to my friend Chris as I lamented once again my seeming lack of progress transforming into the mature woman of God I had imagined I would be. "When God is done fixing me, I want to be calm, quiet, and wise like her."

As I told Chris more about my frustration, my sweet friend listened well, as she always did, until the steady stream of words stopped, and I paused to take a breath.

"Whatever God's perfect plans are for you, Kelly, I can't imagine they will involve you being calm and quiet," she said gently, eyes twinkling and a kind smile on her face. "Whatever God has planned for you will be the perfect match for your loud, enthusiastic, bubbling, passionate personality. God didn't make you calm and quiet. God made you in a different way and I'm so glad He did. You aren't supposed to be like Judy; you are meant to be you."

I have returned to that conversation repeatedly whenever I find myself wishing I was more like someone else. My friend reminded me God created me with a particular Kelly-shaped blueprint in mind. God gave me a combination of strengths, talents, and personality characteristics unlike any other of His creations. While we are each made in the image of our God, we express the variety and beauty of that image in a myriad of ways. My job is to express the "Kelly-ness" of God.

We are often tempted to look around and see others who seem to have what we want. I envied my friend Judy's quiet wisdom and thoughtful demeanor, thinking it was "holier" than my more ebullient style of communicating. Yet, in the years since I received my friend Chris's encouragement, I see how God has used my gifts in a different way, even as I learn from Judy's quieter example. Judy and I ended up working together at our church, and I saw firsthand how our styles complemented each other, with God using our differences to build up His people in more ways than would have been accomplished had we been more alike.

Chris gave me a precious gift the day she chose to encourage me and name me well. She saw my unique gifts, affirmed God's work in my life, and expressed her love and affection for me—the real me, the person God made like no other. When we call out the best in one another, we hear God's voice more clearly.

While we are each invited into a process of transformation to hone and refine the best of our gifts, we are never asked to become a replica of someone else or a version of ourselves that bears no resemblance to our authentic selves. As we embark on the journey toward personal growth and spiritual maturity, learning from our mistakes and finishing the rough edges, we are wise to return to God and others who name us well as we decide how our strengths and interests coincide with our unique place in God's kingdom.

1. Who have you admired and wished you could be more like?
2. What characteristics do you admire in them?
3. How can you learn from them, yet still embrace your own unique gifts? How would embracing your own gifts make you braver?

Prayer: Loving God, hold me close when jealousy rears its ugly head and help me do the hard work to determine why I am feeling envious. Are those feelings because I am not embracing my own gifts or because the object of my jealousy is bravely going down a path I too wish to explore? Show me where the healing lies and how to get there with Your wise help. Thank You for loving friends who name us well and help us be that friend to others. Amen.

Day 20

Then Thomas (also known as Didymus) said to the rest of the disciples, "Let us also go, that we may die with him."

—John 11:16

"No, we don't know, Lord," Thomas said. "We have no idea where you are going, so how can we know the way?"

—John 14:5 NLT

Now Thomas (also known as Didymus), one of the Twelve, was not with the disciples when Jesus came. So the other disciples told him, "We have seen the Lord!" But he said to them, "Unless I see the nail marks in his hands and put my finger where the nails were, and put my hand into his side, I will not believe."

—John 20:24-25

Being honest about how we feel and asking for what we need are sometimes difficult but always brave.

In today's verses, we see three snapshots of the disciple sometimes referred to as "Doubting Thomas."

- In John 11, we see a lionhearted Thomas leading the charge as Jesus tells the disciples they are going to "awaken" His friend Lazarus. Although the other disciples are fearful of returning to Judea, where Jesus has recently been threatened, Thomas urges them to action and solidarity behind their beloved Master. Thomas is willing to die with Jesus, and his courage inspires his comrades to a similar level of commitment.

- In John 14, Jesus has gathered the increasingly confused disciples in an upper room to celebrate the Passover. As Jesus gently breaks the news of His impending death, Thomas asks the question weighing heavily on all their minds, prompting Jesus to reassure them that He is "the way, the truth, and the life" (v. 6).
- In John 20, a brokenhearted and embittered Thomas won't allow himself to hope as he grapples with the tremendous loss they have just experienced. Although his friends insist they have seen the risen Lord, Thomas declares he won't believe them unless he sees proof. A week later, Jesus lovingly looks him in the eye, offers Thomas the evidence of His scars, and says, "Stop doubting and believe" (v. 27).

Whether full of confidence, questions, or doubt, Thomas doesn't hesitate to speak from the heart. Although we have made him the cautionary poster child of doubt, I am reassured and encouraged by the humanity of his reaction in the final story. He left everything to follow this man who he believed to be the Messiah and then watched Jesus and the dreams He represented die on the cross. When presented with the possibility of hope, Thomas honestly asks for what he needs in order to believe.

Just as He did with Thomas, Jesus meets us right where we are with no judgment. No matter the state of our heart, our efforts at hiding behind a mask of propriety are wasted as we draw near to the God who is all-knowing and all-seeing. We are made stronger when we come to God honestly and allow Him to heal our hurts, answer our questions, and give us courage to do the same with the people we love. Owning our feelings, asking for what we need, and sharing our authentic selves require a willingness to dig deeper and take risks. In that place of transparency, God can and will work miracles.

1. Do you ever find yourself hiding your feelings or presenting a more "holy" version of yourself when you talk with God?
2. What would it be like to be completely honest with God about your hurt, jealousy, fears, doubts, and other difficult feelings?
3. If you haven't already, read the entirety of John 11, 14, and 20 to learn more about Thomas. Notice that Jesus never calls him "Doubting Thomas." If you were to choose a different adjective to put in front of Thomas's name, what would it be?

Prayer: Father, sometimes we feel as if we should hide from You until we get ourselves together. Just like King David in the Psalms, we can come to You just as we are: angry, jealous, confused, worried, or full of doubt. Our authentic self is safe with You, and You have the power to heal us, guide us, and answer our questions. We are fully known and fully loved by You. Amen.

Being Brave
Is Being Vulnerable

Day 21

But he said to me, "My grace is sufficient for you, for my power is made perfect in weakness." Therefore I will boast all the more gladly about my weaknesses, so that Christ's power may rest on me.

—2 Corinthians 12:9

Now that I, your Lord and Teacher, have washed your feet, you also should wash one another's feet.

—John 13:14

Being brave is being vulnerable.

By definition, *vulnerable* means "capable of being wounded." In recent years, I have learned volumes about the bravery of vulnerability from my friends at The Lamb Center.

The Lamb Center, where I have been volunteering since 2008, is a local day shelter for homeless and poor individuals in our community. The Lamb Center guests have access to breakfast and lunch, as well as showers and laundry services. Dedicated staff and volunteers are there to assist those who visit to access other services they might need, such as health care, mental health services, job placement, and veterans' benefits. The Lamb Center offers two Bible studies every day, and the community gathers to pray six times a day. While Bible study and prayer are always optional, the care given to each individual who walks through the door is offered with the hope they will know how very much God loves them.

The Lamb Center is a place of radical hospitality for those who are struggling to find hope in desperate circumstances. I lead the Tuesday afternoon Bible study, and I am humbled by the honesty and vulnerability I experience around the table each week. My friends at The Lamb Center are under no delusions or misconceptions that they have their lives under control. The pride and arrogance that plague many of us with comfortable homes and money in the bank have long since been left behind by my friends who sleep in the woods. Unlike many of us in more affluent circumstances, they know they need help because their circumstances leave them no alternative. Around this holy table, the masks of invincibility are left outside. When you have nothing left to lose, you have nothing left to hide.

Being vulnerable is the hardest part of being brave for many of us. We are afraid to appear weak. We avoid taking risks because we fear looking foolish or getting hurt. We resist asking for help at all costs, not wanting to admit we can't handle the challenges of life with ease. Authenticity and vulnerability are closely linked as we pretend to be someone we are not in order to appear stronger, more capable, and more in control than we really are. To be vulnerable is to lower the shield we use to protect ourselves from a world that might judge us and ultimately reject us.

During Holy Week one year, I participated in a foot-washing observance at The Lamb Center. Following Jesus's example in John 13, I had the privilege of washing the feet of some of my friends. What I found to be much more difficult was allowing one of my friends to kneel in front of me and wash my feet in return. Taking off my shoes and socks, I allowed my friend Patti to tenderly hold my feet in her hands. As she lovingly washed and dried each foot while praying a blessing over me, I found the experience to be simultaneously awkward and holy, embarrassingly intimate and sweet. I had tears in my eyes the entire time. Although I felt vulnerable, I was moved by the connection I experienced with our servant Lord and with my sister who loves me.

Jesus showed us the power of vulnerability by taking on the role of a servant and kneeling to wash the dusty feet of His disciples. In His humility, Jesus showed us His strength and told us to go and do likewise. When we are on our knees in front of another, literally or figuratively, we have no choice but to turn our gaze upward. We were created to need one another, but first we must reach out and say, "Here I am."

Being vulnerable is part of being brave.

1. What does the word *vulnerable* mean to you? What situations make you feel the most vulnerable?
2. Do you agree that being vulnerable is part of being brave? Why or why not?
3. What freedom is found in the statement: "When you have nothing left to lose, you have nothing left to hide"?

Prayer: Tender, loving Lord, Your example of servanthood reminds us of the power of taking care of one another from a position of humility. Help us find ways to serve one another, and remind us of the beauty of the words one another *as we learn to receive as well as give. Open our hearts in the next few days to the gifts of vulnerability and the part it plays in our journey of being brave. Amen.*

Day 22

For it is by grace you have been saved, through faith—and this is not from yourselves, it is the gift of God—not by works, so that no one can boast.

—Ephesians 2:8-9

And I am sure that God who began the good work within you will keep right on helping you grow in his grace until his task within you is finally finished on that day when Jesus Christ returns.

—Philippians 1:6 TLB

Some days, as the day draws to a close, I feel like a complete failure. Not every day, but on more days than I would like to admit, I reach the end of the day feeling dissatisfied. I find myself wrestling with a nagging sense of disappointment, disillusionment, and discontent with the items left unchecked on my to-do list and the expectations I had for myself that I didn't meet.

I got the bills paid, but the laundry is half finished. I made the phone calls and sent the e-mails I needed to send but didn't get in any of the writing time I had planned. I spent some time in prayer but never got around to exercising. I called the friend who has been on my mind but never called my mom back. I got through the difficult conversation with my friend without losing my temper, but then I snapped in frustration at the customer service person at the cable company.

And, of course, I *still* didn't tackle all the piles and clean out all the closets, cupboards, laundry room, file cabinet, and so on, which I have been threatening to clean out for ~~months~~ years. My mess is still a mess.

If I think about the disappointment in my day, an expectation of perfection is at the heart of the issue. Simply put, it seems I am disappointed that I still haven't figured out a way to do everything perfectly.

How much is enough? What percentage of my expectations for myself do I need to meet in order to be satisfied? How much of my avoiding, numbing, procrastinating behavior is related to striving for the unattainable and continually setting myself up for failure?

But . . .

Is the alternative to just give up and settle for mediocrity? If I don't at least try to improve in the areas where I struggle, am I living up to the potential placed within me by my Creator? How do I find the balance of good enough?

And here, right here, is where many of us get stuck.

We answer the seductive call of perfection with comparison and competition, depression and denial, rationalizations and reasons why tomorrow will be different. Many of us know in our heart we are saved by grace alone and that our worth is found in our identity as beloved children of God, but the discontent remains. We still aren't good enough.

We still aren't perfect.

But we don't want anyone else to find out, so we share our shiny moments on social media or in the hallways at work, school, or church, and we stuff the rest under the bed. We feel lonely because we think we are the only one with a bunch of crap hidden behind a dust ruffle.

I think it is safe to say I am not going to figure out how to be perfect in this lifetime. In fact, I am beginning to understand that discontent and even failure help me grow and move closer to living the values I claim are important to me. My life is a beautiful mess, full of great joy and frequent struggles. Most days, I am at peace with that truth. Other days . . . other days I find myself back in that cycle of disappointment and wonder if I am the only one.

1. Do you ever feel disappointed with your performance? How does perfectionism keep you stuck?
2. How do you find a balance between striving for excellence and striving for perfection? When does good enough become good enough?
3. What have you learned from the places you fall short? How do you deal with failure?

Prayer: God, help me remember there is nothing I can do to earn Your love and nothing I can do to lose Your love. When I fail, You are always there to forgive me and help me start over. Remind me, on the days I am disappointed with myself, I am a masterpiece unfolding and a work in progress. You want the best for me and won't give up until You have completed the work You have begun. Struggling well is part of the journey. Help me be patient and keep my eyes on You. Amen.

Day 23

Admit your faults to one another and pray for each other so that you may be healed. The earnest prayer of a righteous man has great power and wonderful results.

—James 5:16 TLB

For where two or three are gathered in my name, there am I among them.

—Matthew 18:20 ESV

Maintaining the illusion of having it all together is exhausting, and living our lives online doesn't help.

With the advent of our social media culture, those of us who participate feed the skewed perceptions others have about us by what we post, such as our most attractive photos and our most noteworthy accomplishments. While I am quick to share my girls' prom photos and college acceptances, the hard days slip by without mention. Although the highlight reel of our life is accessible to my 702 Facebook friends, only those closest to our family know that one of my daughters cried practically every single day in middle school because middle school stinks and mean girls are mean. When one of my girls suffered from crippling anxiety and depression during high school, only our inner circle knew our fear, worry, and triumphs as we sought help and eventually crawled our way back out of that dark hole. Online, our life looks perfect.

Don't get me wrong, I love the community and camaraderie of Facebook and other social media platforms. As long as we remember that much of what we see online is only a tiny sliver of reality, it is a wonderful place to share, connect, and celebrate our lives together. It is when we hold up our real, messy lives for comparison to that highlight reel of someone else's online life that we may find ourselves in trouble.

It would not be appropriate to share many of our personal struggles on social media or with casual acquaintances. Yet this cleaned-up, online version of other people's lives is the very thing that contributes to many of us feeling as if we are the only ones who struggle. While it seems as if everyone else's kid is thriving, ours is struggling. While it seems as if everyone else has a perfect marriage, we are still searching for our Prince Charming. While it seems as if everyone else is going on fabulous vacations and being invited to interesting social events, we are trying to get the laundry done, pay the bills, and take care of our aging parents. Life just looks easier for everyone else, and sometimes that perception doesn't feel very fair.

If, in the interest of looking like I have it all together, I only share my life at the "online" level of honesty and vulnerability, then I am missing out on the opportunity for real-life intimacy and friendship. If I spend more time online than I do face-to-face with my loved ones, then I am apt to have an unrealistic perception of what is normal. Settling for online intimacy is like eating a candy bar when what I need is a healthy meal. My hunger is temporarily satisfied, but my need for nourishment is not.

To combat this tendency, I get together with a group of women every other Friday. There are nine of us, and most of us are a year or two on either side of our fiftieth birthdays. Our kids are all teens or twenty-somethings, and we have all been married for approximately forever. If we don't run out of time telling stories and laughing, we end our time by praying together. We have traveled a number of difficult roads together, from kids with chronic illness or legal problems to aging parents with Alzheimer's or cancer. We have stood with one another through our own health challenges and through the loss of too many of our parents. Talking, laughing, crying, and praying with these ladies feels like church to me, in all the best ways.

Several years ago, our little group got very busy with life and fell out of the habit of meeting regularly. We were lamenting about this sad state of affairs in a Facebook chat stream in which we found ourselves "meeting" instead. One friend mentioned she missed our face-to-face time together and wasn't willing to put it on a back burner anymore. We all agreed we needed to make it a priority. We needed our "intentional girl time!" From that moment on, IGT was the official name for our gatherings.

These women, and other people whom I feel closest to in my life, are the ones who love me even though they know the real me—my faults and my fears, my worries and my insecurities, my doubts and my struggles. They know the me I don't share on social media. They are also more likely to be those with whom I regularly pray because of our shared belief that we don't have all the answers and we don't have to carry the burden alone. They are my lifeline and my sanctuary. They keep me connected to God.

1. Do you participate in social media? If so, what do you see as the advantages and disadvantages?
2. How does comparing your life with others get in the way of intimacy?
3. Do you have people in your life whom you regularly ask to pray for you? If not, how could you begin to form a group of prayer partners whom you trust?

Prayer: Loving Father, help us always remember that nobody has a perfect life. Comparison gets in the way of connection and compassion, and we need the community that is created by remembering we all belong to one another. Make us aware of those opportunities around us to pray for and with those You have placed in our lives. Help us find a healthy balance in our use of social media and remind us of our need for face-to-face friendships. Amen.

Day 24

She gave this name to the LORD who spoke to her: "You are the God who sees me," for she said, "I have now seen the One who sees me."

—Genesis 16:13

And the Lord God said, "It isn't good for man to be alone; I will make a companion for him, a helper suited to his needs."

—Genesis 2:18 TLB

There is healing magic in the words *me too*.

We yearn for connection. We are wired for belonging. We want to know we are not traveling this path alone. Right from the beginning, God spoke these words, "It is not good for man to be alone," and ordained our hunger for community. We need each other.

Yet, at the same time, we hide from each other. We push each other away in the spaces we need each other most. The nagging voice of our inner critic whispers these words:

- *You have nothing meaningful to offer.*
- *You aren't as good as ______.*
- *You aren't as smart as ______.*
- *You are not enough ______.*
- *If they really knew you, they wouldn't love you.*

So, we pretend. We wear our shiny, happy masks and insist we are "fine." We adamantly declare how very busy we are as our proof of worthiness. We compare and compete, hoping to catch up and earn entrance to an imaginary club for which there are no actual members, Club Perfect. We are convinced we just need to try harder so we won't be the only one on the outside looking in.

But perhaps, in our loneliness, we begin to experiment. We find a few people with whom we drop the act momentarily. We take a few risks and test the waters. We admit our struggles:

- *Sometimes I wonder if I'm doing it all wrong.*
- *Sometimes I wonder if God is listening to my prayers.*
- *Sometimes being a parent/child/spouse/friend is really, really hard.*
- *Sometimes I wonder if I'll ever get over my bad habit of ______.*
- *Sometimes I feel like a total failure.*

And then we hear those magical, beautiful, life-giving words . . .

Me too!

We find we are not alone after all! We realize we are not the only one who wonders or the only one who doubts. We recognize ourselves in the stories others share and offer our own gift of *me too*. We discover our inner critics speak a similar language, and we begin to suspect it is a language of lies. Perhaps, instead, the opposite is true:

- *I am not the only one who struggles.*
- *I do have something to offer.*
- *We are all imperfect, growing, learning, and changing.*

- *We are stronger when we stand together.*
- *I showed up, I allowed my authentic self to be seen, and I was loved anyway.*

Most of us don't need others to fix our struggles, our worries, our doubts, or our fears. We don't need advice, platitudes, or solutions. Often, we already know the answers or the path to find them. We simply need to know we are not alone in our struggles. We want to know we have been seen. We need to hear *me too*.

By saying yes to the cross, Jesus came to help us find the path back to the Kingdom for which we were made. In the original garden, we lived in perfect connection and community with one another and with God. Before we listened to the lies, we were safe and we were known. No hiding, no pretending, no blaming, no rationalizations, no fig leaves to cover our shame. We started listening to the lies, and we got separated from one another and from God. Through His brave choice to make Himself vulnerable to the executioner's nails, Jesus provides us the way back home.

We need one another. Take a risk, let down your guard, and speak your truth. Show up and let yourself be seen. Offer the gift of *me too* to your fellow strugglers and take the hand of your brave Savior who leads the way back home.

1. What makes it difficult or scary to be real with other people?
2. Who are the people in your life with whom you can speak authentically, the people who get the most frequent glimpses

of the real you and offer you the gift of *me too*? Thank God for them today and then reach out to them and thank them for being your *me too* people.

3. Read the entire story of Hagar in Genesis 16. How does it feel to know that our God is a God who sees you? What is so meaningful about truly being seen by God and by others?

Prayer: Thank You, God, for the precious gift of me too. *Thank You for being the God who sees each one of us and gives us the ability to truly see and be seen by one another. Help me be brave enough to share enough of myself that others will be able to both give and receive* me too*'s. I am grateful for the people in my life who remind me I am not alone in my struggles. Help me love others in such a way that they too will know they have a friend. Amen.*

Day 25

A woman in that town who lived a sinful life learned that Jesus was eating at the Pharisee's house, so she came there with an alabaster jar of perfume. As she stood behind him at his feet weeping, she began to wet his feet with her tears. Then she wiped them with her hair, kissed them and poured perfume on them.

—*Luke 7:37-38*

Jesus wept.

—*John 11:35*

I cry in church fairly often. I'm not talking about weeping or sobbing, but I regularly find myself discreetly wiping away a tear or two during worship services. For me, this is usually a good thing and means that something is connecting for me deeply and the Holy Spirit is at work.

I remember one occasion, however, when I was struggling to hold it together and had to dig through my purse for tissues in an attempt to gain control. It was during a Sunday evening service at our new church only a few months after we started attending. For some reason, I had come to church by myself that day, so I was sitting alone. Leaving our old church had been heartbreaking for me, and I was still feeling somewhat fragile and guarded. That evening something the pastor said spoke so directly to my broken places that I was momentarily overwhelmed by God's presence. I felt grateful to have this place to worship and grateful that I hadn't given up on church. Through my tears, I silently thanked God for the music, the people, and the centuries of Christians who had gone before me, trying to figure out how to be the church. My heart was full to overflowing as I considered all these stumbling, failing, broken people, each getting it wrong over and over again, and yet, somehow still getting it right often enough that God keeps showing up in the midst of our beautiful mess.

In that moment, I was overcome by the extravagance of God's grace and the feeling I might possibly have found a new church home. Although I attempted to hide my tears, my struggle was mostly in vain. After the service was over, thinking I had straightened myself up and looked calm, cool, and collected, I reached down to get my purse and looked up to find myself face-to-face with a lovely lady who had a kind smile on her face.

"Can I give you a hug?" she said.

Feeling awkward and embarrassed at having been caught in such a vulnerable moment, I started to launch into an explanation of how these were mostly happy tears and I was just fine. I didn't need her to comfort me or fix me. Then, I stopped myself.

And I simply said, "I would love a hug. Thank you."

In the final weeks of His earthly ministry, Jesus encountered another broken woman moved by emotion. The woman described in Luke 7 as weeping at Jesus's feet, unlike me, seemed unashamed of her tears. She was overwhelmed with gratitude and love but unconcerned by the crowd of witnesses, and her tears flowed freely as she shared the depth of her heart with her Lord. Her tears became her offering as she tenderly knelt before Jesus and kissed His feet. I wish Scripture gave us more details about what she said as she wept, but I suspect Jesus heard her whisper, "Thank you," more than once. Even as others in attendance scoffed at her sacrifice, Jesus acknowledged and commended her tears as proof of her "great love" and as an example for the others around them.

Although I often struggle with moments like these, embracing instead of avoiding strong emotion is a brave and vulnerable choice. While our tears sometimes feel like an unwelcome loss of control, we are created to feel deeply, and Jesus honors those moments when we come to Him and to each other with our broken, humble hearts overflowing.

1. What is difficult about allowing others to see us in a moment of emotion?
2. What type of emotion usually brings tears to your eyes? Do you cry easily or rarely? How do you feel about your tears when they come?
3. What do you imagine Jesus said to the woman in today's verse in response to her tears? Would you be willing to consider Him saying something similar to you?

Prayer: Strong Father, teach me to cherish tears and fragility as a sign I am human. Emotions can sometimes make me feel weak, yet I know anything that draws me closer to You ultimately makes me stronger. Teach me to lean on You in my weakness and come to You with all the feelings I am experiencing. As the childhood song says, "Jesus loves me this I know, for the Bible tells me so. Little ones to Him belong, they are weak and He is strong." Thank You for the gift of our emotions. Amen.

Day 26

There is no fear in love. But perfect love drives out fear, because fear has to do with punishment. The one who fears is not made perfect in love.

—*1 John 4:18*

"The most important one," answered Jesus, "is this: 'Hear, O Israel: The Lord our God, the Lord is one. Love the Lord your God with all your heart and with all your soul and with all your mind and with all your strength.' The second is this: 'Love your neighbor as yourself.' There is no commandment greater than these."

—*Mark 12:29-31*

"What does it mean when it says perfect love drives out fear?" I asked this question to the thoughtful group of Bible study participants as we gathered around the table at The Lamb Center. We were studying some of the many places in Scripture that talk about fear and courage. At this point in our discussion, we had landed in one of today's verses: "Where God's love is, there is no fear, because God's perfect love drives out fear" (1 John 4:18 NCV).

It was an active group, and many around the table had offered insights and stories about their own journey with fear and their attempts at bravery. When I asked this question about perfect love driving out fear, one of the newer ladies to our company shared these thoughts:

> I was so scared. I had gotten sick and lost everything. I ended up in the hospital, and when it was time to leave, I didn't have anywhere to go. One of the people at the hospital told me about The Lamb Center. When I came here, people were so nice. Everyone showed me the love of God. The more I felt the love of God through the people here, the less afraid I felt. I didn't feel alone anymore. Experiencing God's love through this place drove out my fear. That's what it means when it says perfect love drives out fear.

My friends at The Lamb Center know firsthand about fear. They fear having no place to go. They fear sleeping at a bus stop or in the woods. They fear an approaching storm when they have no shelter. Every day, they struggle with the fear of disconnection, judgment, shame, and loss. They routinely face the fear of isolation and the fear of losing hope and never finding it again. My friends at The Lamb Center know all about what it means to dig deep for the courage to face their fears.

Fear and anxiety are part of the human journey. While I am grateful my fears don't include worrying about where I will sleep, I understand the solace of realizing I am not alone in my struggle, whatever that struggle might be. Each of us around the table that day could relate to the need to navigate the difficult paths of fear, worry, and anxiety, and we were all grateful God seemed to have some answers for us in His word—answers that often, it seems, include our need to share our lives with one another.

God says over and over again in Scripture, "Do not fear, for I am with you" (see Isaiah 41:10). God's consistent answer to our fears is

His presence. Often, God's presence involves our presence with one another. Perfect love casts out fear. God's love is made perfect when we reach out and love one another, especially in the hard places.

Jesus tells us the greatest commandment is this: Love God and love one another (see Matthew 22:36-39). Could loving one another with the love of God be the antidote to fear?

1. What do you think it means when it says perfect love drives out fear? Does a specific experience come to mind when you hear the phrase?
2. What comforts you when you are feeling fearful or anxious? How do you ask for help?
3. In the next few days, look for opportunities to offer God's perfect love to someone who is struggling with fear and anxiety. As you watch for your chance to do so, think about what that kind of love might look like.

Prayer: Jesus, help us be brave enough to love one another well and to lean on one another in the difficult spaces. Help us recognize fear in its many disguises, such as anger or despair. Remind us we are never alone, for You are always with us. Help us be Your comforting presence with one another. When all else fails and we don't know what to do, help us remember the greatest commandment: Love God and love one another. We love You so much, Lord. Amen.

Day 27

Then Mary said, "I am willing to be used of the Lord. Let it happen to me as you have said."

—Luke 1:38 NLV

Near the cross of Jesus stood his mother, his mother's sister, Mary the wife of Clopas, and Mary Magdalene. When Jesus saw his mother there, and the disciple whom he loved standing nearby, he said to her, "Woman, here is your son," and to the disciple, "Here is your mother." From that time on, this disciple took her into his home.

—John 19:25-27

There is nothing more difficult than watching your child suffer.

When my younger daughter was in high school, she was diagnosed with an anxiety disorder after struggling for months with debilitating panic attacks. Although we eventually found the right course of treatment for her, her junior year in high school was a nightmare for our family. Watching her struggle and being unable to take away her pain was excruciating, and my stomach was continually in knots. For a time, we lived with constant uneasiness and watched her closely for any sign she might be in danger. I struggled to find a balance between hovering over her, constantly taking her emotional temperature, and giving her some space and privacy like a normal teenager. I reminded her again and again God was right smack in the middle of this process with us.

Every day was an occasion for prayer, and every day a reason for gratitude. We believed in the professionals who guided us, we believed in the process of healing, and we believed in her. With our help, with God's help, Brooke courageously fought her way back and is now a healthy, happy college student. She is one of the bravest people I know.

When we love someone deeply, we open ourselves up to the probability of pain, heartache, and loss. By caring for another, we make the brave and vulnerable choice to allow ourselves to be hurt. While many of us consider the rewards of loving someone worth the risks, others find the cost too high and the wounds from previous relationships too deep. Protecting our heart by remaining cautiously at a distance often seems the safer choice.

From the minute Mary received the news from Gabriel of her impending motherhood, she must have wondered what her future held. While she may have dreamed of being a mother, I suspect being the unmarried mother of the Messiah was not something she had ever imagined. Although this baby and the circumstances of His birth were unique, I believe Mary felt the same fierce protectiveness any mother feels the moment she first held Him in her arms. As Jesus grew to adulthood, His destiny unfolded, and the inevitability of the cross began to come into focus, I can only imagine the firestorm of emotions swirling in Mary's heart. How could this be God's plan for her baby boy? What could she do to keep Him safe?

Yet, when the time came, there she stood. Instead of turning away to soften the searing pain in her heart, Mary stood resolutely at the foot of the cross staring into the face of her beloved child as He suffered and died. No one would have blamed her had she waited and watched from a distance, but she made the brave choice to wade into the horror and share in His suffering by standing watch. In His final moments, when Jesus made John promise to care for her in His absence, she must have wondered how she would ever survive this excruciating pain and loss. I wish Scripture told us more about their reunion three days later!

I can't begin to compare my journey as a mother to Mary's, yet each of us who enters into the suffering of another knows that loving deeply is hard, holy, and brave work. There is no safe way to love, but the joy of connection is worth the cost. Through our relationships with one another, we more fully experience the love God has for us.

1. Has there been a time you guarded your heart and pulled back from a relationship because you were scared of being hurt?
2. How does trusting God impact your ability to trust others? How does trusting others impact your ability to trust God?
3. Scripture tells us several other women were standing with Mary at the foot of the cross. What do you imagine they did to support her in this unbelievably difficult situation?

Prayer: Loving Father, sometimes it is hard to love other people well. When someone we love is suffering, we want to fix the problem and take away the pain. Give us the strength and courage to stand watch like Mary—to bear witness in the face of suffering instead of running away when it hurts too much. Remind us that our presence in times of difficulty is enough because Your presence when we gather in Your name is enough. Thank You for giving us the capacity to love one another and help us to love like You do. Amen.

PART 3

Self-Discipline

For God has not given us a spirit of fear and timidity, but of power, love and SELF-DISCIPLINE.

—2 Timothy 1:7 NLT

In the various biblical translations, this third aspect of the Spirit God has given us is translated in several different ways: self-discipline, self-control, sound judgment, and sound mind. Developing *self-discipline* is part of growing up into our best selves. As we partner with God by showing up and participating in the work He is doing in our lives, we gain emotional and spiritual maturity. We work like it is all up to us and pray like it is all up to God, getting clearer about the role we play in the masterpiece we are cocreating with God. God is ready to empower us with all we need to be brave, but we must show up and do the work. In this section, we will explore what it means to be *engaged* in the world and *empowered* by the Holy Spirit, experiencing the freedom and joy of living the life God dreams for us.

Being Brave
Is Being Engaged

Day 28

David also said to Solomon his son, "Be strong and courageous, and **do the work**. *Do not be afraid or discouraged, for the LORD God, my God, is with you."*

—1 Chronicles 28:20, emphasis added

For I can do everything through Christ, who gives me strength.

—Philippians 4:13 NLT

Being brave is being engaged.

When my older daughter, Alexandra, was six years old, she decided she wanted to learn to Hula-Hoop. She had not previously used a Hula-Hoop, and I can't recall from where the inspiration came that particular day. Wherever this urge originated, she made up her mind she was going to learn to Hula-Hoop, and she was going to learn it immediately.

And Hula-Hoop she did.

She took her Hula-Hoop and parked herself in the cul-de-sac in front of our house, right at the end of our driveway. Over the next several hours, with me checking on her from time to time, she taught herself to twirl it. At first, she had very little success, and the hoop fell instantly to the ground. Each time, she would pick it up and try again, often with a confident smile on her face, sometimes with a determined frown. Eventually, she began to gain momentum as she kept the

Hula-Hoop moving for a few seconds, then a whole minute. By the end of the day, she was able to spin the hoop around her waist and eventually around her arm. Over the course of the following summer, she would often walk around the cul-de-sac with the hoop spinning confidently off various parts of her body, beaming proudly at her hard-won skill.

Alexandra had an idea she wanted to try, a new skill she wanted to learn. Instead of doing research, thinking about it, talking about it with friends, worrying about how it would turn out, and convincing herself she would likely fail, she just grabbed her Hula-Hoop and set to work.

Now a confident young adult, Alexandra continues to inspire me with her work ethic and quiet determination. Needing little applause or accolades from others to keep her focused, she is self-motivated and curious about the world around her and the ways in which her unique gifts might contribute. In describing my older daughter, I often tell people I admire her steely resolve. Alexandra sets her mind to a project and then she gets it done. As a person prone to overthinking, procrastination, and a need for applause, I have the utmost admiration for her willingness to jump in and do the work required to accomplish her dreams. She is not successful every time, but she rarely suffers from regrets about not giving her best effort. Alexandra engages with the world and goes after what she wants. She is one of the bravest people I know.

As we have discovered in our study, numerous passages in Scripture remind us to be courageous and strong. God knows we are sometimes fearful and in need of encouragement, so reminders of His presence are scattered throughout the Bible. However, in today's first verse, David reminds his son Solomon of one other important ingredient of being brave: we must do the work.

Do the work. Other translations say *get to* work (CEV, ISV, TLB). Still other versions tell us David instructed Solomon to be "strong and courageous and act" (NRSV, NASB).

Just do it. Get involved. Create something. Make a difference. Jump in. Tell your story. Engage with the world.

Get up and do the next right thing.

There are no shortcuts. Part of being brave is engaging with the world around us, taking a leap, and getting involved. The world is full of writers who don't write, painters who don't paint, and dancers who don't dance. We will never know what we might be able to do, if we never do the work to make it happen. Action is required to make our dreams come true, but sometimes getting started is the hardest part. Once we start, once we take the first brave step forward, the biggest obstacle will be behind us.

Grab your Hula-Hoop . . .

Being engaged is part of being brave.

1. What does the word *engaged* mean to you? How would you define it, and who are some examples of people who are engaged?
2. What obstacles do you experience when you try to engage in a new way? Fear, doubt, lack of support, worry about results?

3. What is one thing you would try if you knew you could not fail?

Prayer: Father of possibilities, our hearts quicken when we dream of the thing we have not yet had the courage to begin. Lead us one step down the path of possibilities and show us the next right thing. Give us the courage and the self-discipline it will require to get to work. With Your help, we can do hard things. We can do new things. We can do brave things. Whisper in our ear when we hesitate. In You, all things are possible. Amen.

Day 29

"For I know the plans I have for you," declares the Lord, *"plans to prosper you and not to harm you, plans to give you hope and a future. Then you will call on me and come and pray to me, and I will listen to you. You will seek me and find me when you seek me with all your heart."*

—Jeremiah 29:11-13

Little children, let us stop just saying *we love people; let us* really *love them, and* show *it by our* actions.

—1 John 3:18 TLB

When my girls were tiny, a neighbor invited me to a women's Bible study at her church. Frankly, she had my full attention and grateful acquiescence the minute she said the words *free child care*. Being the parent of little people made me tired, so free child care was all I needed to hear before saying yes to almost anything in those early years.

Months turned into years, and I found my participation in these Bible studies to be a much-needed source of connection, community, and intellectual stimulation. Digging around in these ancient texts and meeting together with others similarly engaged were lifelines for me, socially, emotionally, intellectually, and spiritually. Eventually, we started offering similar Bible studies (and free child care) at my own church, and I became more and more captivated by God's word.

However, after several years, I began to get restless. I was leading

Bible studies, teaching Sunday school, and doing all manner of other "church lady" activities. I was teaching my kids about Jesus, inviting my neighbors to Bible study, and making an occasional casserole. I was praying regularly and trying to cultivate the famous fruit of the spirit: love, joy, peace, patience, kindness, goodness, faithfulness, gentleness, and self-control (Galatians 5:22-23). Wasn't this what I was supposed to be doing? I didn't understand why I had this nagging sense of discontent.

Here was the problem: the more I immersed myself in the Scriptures, particularly the things that Jesus said, the more I began to suspect that I might be missing the point. Apparently, being comfortable and happy was not the ultimate goal. My personal salvation was only part of the story. Feeling all the warm and fuzzy feelings was a lovely by-product of faith but not the reason Jesus came. Jesus wasn't just talking about blessing the blessed. He was preaching about radical, hard things like feeding the hungry, clothing the naked, loving my enemies, and binding up the brokenhearted. Jesus loved and spent time with the poor, the unclean, and the sinners.

I was hanging out with middle-class church ladies just like me.

What was I to do with this confusion, discomfort, and dissatisfaction? What did God expect me to do with these difficult things Jesus was saying? Why couldn't I just be satisfied doing what I had been doing?

In spring 2008, I was still wrestling with God and paralyzed by my need to have a blueprint of just what exactly God was up to in my life. To be honest, Jesus's words were starting to wreck my comfortable Christianity. I had been perfectly happy in the safety of my suburban church, and then I wasn't. Then, I read these words in the Bible study I was doing: "Our motto should be 'Whatever God says to you, do it.' If you are ready to make this motto your own, write it in the margin. Sign and date it as a reminder of when you made this commitment."[1]

Initially, I wouldn't write those words. I knew God had been pushing me, but I still wasn't clear on His plan. I needed to know what the "whatever" was before I would agree. I needed details. I was comfortable in the safe familiar; why should I sign up for the unknown?

But what else had I learned during my time studying Scripture?

- God has a plan for my life, a plan to give me a hope and a future (Jeremiah 29:11).
- I can be bold and unafraid because God will never leave me or forsake me (Deuteronomy 31:6).
- I will find God when I seek Him with my whole heart (1 Chronicles 28:9).
- God has not given me a spirit of fear or timidity, but a spirit of power and of love and of self-control (2 Timothy 1:7).

If I believed these Scriptures, shouldn't I be willing to trust God, no matter what? Even if I didn't know all the details?

So finally, on May 12, 2008 (I still have the book), I wrote, "Whatever God says to me, I will do it," in the margin and signed it, thinking, *I don't know where You are sending me, Jesus, but I will go. I say yes.*

Two months later, through a series of coincidences completely unrelated, I found my way to The Lamb Center for the first time. Being part of The Lamb Center community has been one of the greatest joys of my life, and God has used this humble place to change me, challenge me, use me, and draw me more deeply into His heart. I see the kingdom of God at work every time I pass through the doors.

God is willing and eager to involve us in His adventures if only we are willing. When I whispered my tremulous yes, God pointed to the door He had already opened for me. God knew right where I belonged.

1. What verses has God used to shake you up or make you uncomfortable?
2. What needs in the world around you break your heart? What wrongs do you want to make right?
3. Considering the questions above, how might you use what God has given you to make a difference in your corner of the world this week?

Prayer: Father, You are already at work in the world, and You are eager to get us more deeply involved. We know we grow stronger and more mature as we step out of our comfort zones, yet sometimes the safe familiar seems better. Show us where in our lives we might take baby steps into the place You could use us to love our hurting world. Our unique voices, experiences, gifts, and passions can be used to comfort someone who is hurting or love someone who feels alone. Make us brave, Lord, and put us to work! Amen.

Note

1. Priscilla Shirer, *Discerning the Voice of God: How to Recognize When God Speaks* (Chicago: Moody, 2012), 106.

Day 30

Do not boast about tomorrow,
for you do not know what a day may bring.

—Proverbs 27:1

If anyone, then, knows the good they ought to do and doesn't do it, it is sin for them.

—James 4:17

I am the Queen of Someday. The Princess of Procrastination.

After all, why do today what can be put off until tomorrow? Or next week?

- Someday, I will call my friend.
- Someday, I will have that difficult conversation I'm avoiding.
- Someday, I will clean out the cabinets, put the photos in an album, and organize our music.
- Someday, I will pray and read my Bible more.
- Someday, I will write a book, audition for a play, paint a painting.
- Someday, I will serve on that committee or give to that ministry.
- Someday, I will feed hungry children, visit the lonely, fight for the oppressed.

Tomorrow, next week, or Someday is *definitely* when all those things will happen.

Someday is seductive. Someday allows me to hold on to the vision I have of myself, the kind of person who I've always wanted to be, the person I've always known I am, and the person who embodies the values I say I have.

I am courageous and adventurous, well traveled and well read, generous and thoughtful, organized and efficient, respected and successful.

Or at least I will be . . . Someday.

Someday keeps my dreams alive.

Someday is rich with promise and possibility but does not require immediate attention. Someday allows one more episode of Netflix, another half hour of Facebook surfing, or another season of prayer for discernment and clarity. Someday is comfortable and safe.

Someday lets me off the hook.

Someday isn't all bad. When my children were babies, we had no money, and I was barely getting through the day, I worshiped at the altar of Someday. Someday kept me sane. Someday, they will sleep through the night. Someday, they will both be potty trained. Someday, they will feed themselves and teach themselves and drive themselves. Someday, I will go to the bathroom by myself. Someday I will have five minutes alone. And, in these cases, thank God, Someday did eventually arrive!

But what if Someday never comes? What if Someday turns into If Only or What If? What if Someday is really just fear?

I recently heard a speaker I admire say, "Someday is a myth." When I heard those words, I felt sucker punched by the betrayal. But what about all my lovely Someday dreams?

Turns out, we are not guaranteed Someday. Since I entered my fifties, the ambiguity of Someday is beginning to feel a little more like giving up and selling out. Although I know dreaming of perfection is unrealistic, settling for Someday is not the answer either. Someday is getting in the way of me finding my brave.

As I think about being brave, I want to be intentional about being truly engaged in the world, a person of action, not just Someday words. I want to live life all-in. I want to stop wasting time on activities that don't reflect my heart. I want to spend my hours in ways that reflect the things I say I believe. I want to avoid cynicism and sideline criticism because they distract me from my goals and give me an excuse to stay stuck in inaction. I want to continue to make progress in my ongoing battle with procrastination, give myself grace, and ask for forgiveness when I slip into old habits. I want to love my people with everything I have to give, even if my tender heart gets broken. I want to pour myself out in service to others and expect nothing in return except the joy of living in the Kingdom. I want to be bold enough to believe my story and my art matter because they are part of the bigger story God is telling. I want to love God with all my heart, soul, mind, and spirit, and love my neighbor as myself. I want to be the change I wish to see in the world.

Maybe, I'm ready for Someday to become Now or Never.

1. In what areas of your life do you find yourself procrastinating? Is perfectionism a part of your procrastination? Or is it fear of failure?
2. Think of one thing you have been planning to do "Someday." If that Someday thing was only available now or never, which would you choose?

3. What is keeping you from doing the Someday thing now? If it isn't possible now, what steps could you take to move closer to making that thing a reality sooner?

Prayer: God of this moment, help me be present now. I don't know how many more days I have left to do the things I dream about doing, so make me brave enough to reject the lure of Someday. The next time I am tempted to put off until another day, whisper in my ear, "Someday is a myth," and give me a nudge in the right direction. I am trusting You will be right beside me as I chase my Someday dream. Make me brave, Lord! Amen.

Day 31

So we fix our eyes not on what is seen, but on what is unseen, since what is seen is temporary, but what is unseen is eternal.

—*2 Corinthians 4:18*

On the first day of the week, very early in the morning, the women took the spices they had prepared and went to the tomb. They found the stone rolled away from the tomb, but when they entered, they did not find the body of the Lord Jesus.

—*Luke 24:1-3*

Last year, I spent several months rewatching all seven seasons of the television series *The West Wing* in my spare time. All 156 episodes. At approximately 45 minutes per episode, that means I spent 117 hours watching *The West Wing*. In all honesty, there is some likelihood I watched *The West Wing* when I should have been doing something a bit more productive.

I have been thinking about the reasons for my *West Wing* devotion/obsession. Beyond the intelligent writing, compelling characters, and peek into the fascinating world of politics, I suspect I am drawn to this show because of the refreshing lack of cynicism.

The West Wing world believes public service, despite the temptations and challenges, is an honorable calling. *The West Wing* world believes good people are drawn to service and sacrifice because they believe that one person, in partnership with other committed people, can make a difference and contribute to making the world a better, safer place of opportunity for all our citizens. Time after time on *The West Wing*, when faced with the expediency of compromised integrity, the characters chose the high road and continued to pursue their goals through diplomacy, creativity, intelligence, hard work, and cooperation. They don't win every battle, but they continue to believe what they are doing is worth the personal sacrifice for the greater good. They don't give up and they never quit trying.

In recent years, in light of ugly partisan politics, evidence of continued systemic racism, an epidemic of mass shootings, and ongoing divisions within the church, I have been struggling not to fall prey to the easy surrender of cynicism. Cynicism says evil and hate are winning and there is nothing we can do about it. Cynicism says people can't ever be trusted to do the right thing. Cynicism says poverty, hunger, violence, and oppression are just part of the world in which we live. Cynicism says that the government, the church, and all other institutions of change are powerless in the face of the selfishness and hard hearts of humans. Cynicism says anyone who believes otherwise is naive at best and possibly downright stupid. Cynicism says our only option is to put our heads down and protect our loved ones.

Cynicism lets us off the hook and absolves us of any responsibility to advocate for change. Cynicism gives us an excuse to stay stuck.

As I think about how easy it is to fall prey to cynicism, I am inspired by the women in today's verse from the Gospel of Luke. Despite the horror of Jesus's crucifixion, they did not run away. After the Sabbath had passed, broken hearts in tow, they chose to prepare spices and journey to the tomb out of a deep love for their Master. At this point in the unfolding story, they believed all was lost and Jesus was gone forever. Several of them had recently stood for hours at the foot of the cross watching the man they believed to be the Messiah die a gruesome death at the hands of their leaders. Yet, despite their grief and confusion over what happened, they moved forward and did the next right thing. They didn't withdraw, give up, or hide behind their sense of powerlessness. They gathered their supplies and set to work. Because of their faithfulness, they were the first to experience their Risen Lord!

Jesus spent His earthly ministry declaring that the kingdom of God is near. God's plan for bringing the kingdom to earth involves our participation, and since the kingdom of God has not yet fully arrived, the work is not yet done. Jesus's band of followers, beginning with those women who found the tomb empty, took His message of love, selflessness, sacrifice, and humility into the world, without the benefit of the internet or mass media. Now 2.9 billion people worldwide call themselves followers of Jesus. I still have hope that people of faith can be part of the solution going forward. If we believe what Jesus says, we are called to be Light in the darkness, even when it is difficult, especially when it is difficult.

Cynicism is the opposite of hope and the opposite of brave. Cynicism says our efforts don't matter. Cynicism says it's not our problem. Cynicism says we may as well give up and quit trying.

Jesus says otherwise.

1. Do you ever struggle with cynicism? If so, how does it affect your willingness to serve in the community?
2. About which issues or causes in our society do you feel passionately? What need do you see in the world around you that draws you in and makes your heart beat faster?
3. What is one action you can take this week to get involved more deeply in something about which you feel passionately? How can you be part of the change you want to see in the world?

Prayer: Hopeful God, heal me of my cynicism. When I slip back into old habits, remind me cynicism is lazy and keeps me stuck. In You, I am a new creation and an agent of change. Make me brave and show me the place where You are calling me to roll up my sleeves and get to work. Help me be the change I want to see in the world, knowing that the seeds I plant of love and hope will ultimately bear fruit under Your loving care. Amen.

Day 32

Shout with joy to the Lord, all the earth!
Worship the Lord with gladness.
Come before him, singing with joy.
Acknowledge that the Lord is God!
He made us, and we are his.
We are his people, the sheep of his pasture.

—Psalm 100:1-3 NLT

Whatever work you do, do it with all your heart. Do it for the Lord and not for men.

—Colossians 3:23 NLV

Several years ago, my older daughter, Alexandra, and I had the privilege of participating in the cast of an original musical. The story and the music for this show were written entirely by my friends Don and Zoe. This particular story, the melodies, and the lyrics were not present in our world prior to Don and Zoe deciding to bring it into existence. Something within them decided that, in a world full of songs and stories, something new was needed, something different, something beautiful, something we didn't know we were missing until we experienced it. As actors, singers, artists, and musicians, we then became part of the creative process by adding our own touch to the story, a collective work of creation that further touched the lives of both the participants and the members of the audience.

Multiply our experience by every song you hear, every play you watch, every book you read, and every piece of artwork you enjoy. What causes someone to decide that the world isn't enough with just the status quo? Why do we build a more beautiful building, sing a different song, paint another painting, write another book? What inspires us to dig deep within ourselves and expose ourselves to criticism and judgment by offering up our creations to public scrutiny?

Although creativity is often associated with more traditional forms of art, such as theatre, music, and painting, the opportunity to look back over the life of Apple cofounder Steve Jobs reminds us creativity occurs anytime we allow ourselves to think outside the confines of that which already exists. Mr. Jobs, in his short life, helped create products we didn't know we needed and now we are sure we can no longer live without. He didn't allow failure to stop him from imagining something new, something better, or something different. Steve Jobs lived his life with an understanding that being in touch with his creativity meant making a difference in the world.

Creating something and offering it to the world is an act of vulnerability. One of my favorite authors, Brené Brown, has written extensively about this topic. She defines vulnerability as "uncertainty, risk and emotional exposure."[1] Vulnerability is when we allow ourselves to show up and be seen with no guarantees of how we or our work will be received. We often view vulnerability as weakness in ourselves and as bravery in others. The question vulnerability and creativity asks of us is this: "What is worth doing even if you fail?"

In a conversation with my daughter and some other friends about the surprising relief of having your worst fears happen and surviving, my daughter and I both told stories of incidents when we were in front of a group of people and failed spectacularly—forgetting the lyrics of a song or freezing entirely and then running off the stage in tears. Yet, she is currently in rehearsals for another play, and I am putting myself in front of an audience once again. Apparently, showing up creatively continues to be worth doing even when we fail.

Creativity is at the heart of what makes us fully alive. On a spiritual level, creativity is our very connection to our Creator—the life force that makes us most like our heavenly Father in whose image we were created. As a person of faith, I recognize that creativity is directly related to staying connected to the originator of that creative spark within me. Knowing that God made each of us with the ability and the yearning to be a creative force within this world challenges me to pay attention to those opportunities I am given to step outside of the status quo and do something different, even when it is scary. My story matters in the larger story that God is telling in our world. Embracing my creativity, in whatever form that might take, is an act of worship and an act of bravery.

1. Do you believe you are a cocreator with God? Why?
2. What does your inner critic tell you about your ability to be creative? If those messages keep you stuck, would you be willing to consider they might be lies?
3. What creative outlets do you have in your life, and in what ways could you nurture that creativity even more?

Prayer: Creator God, what a magnificent world You have made for us! There is so much beauty and so many different ways to express our creativity. Help us see the ways in which You have invited us to use our unique gifts to contribute to the masterpiece You are creating. You ask us to make a joyful noise as we worship You in all that we do. Remind us that we too are creative forces in this world and make us each brave enough to tell our story and sing our song. Amen.

Note

1. Brené Brown, *Daring Greatly: How the Courage to Be Vulnerable Transforms the Way We Live, Love, Parent, and Lead* (New York: Avery, 2015), 36.

Day 33

Am I now trying to win the approval of human beings, or of God? Or am I trying to please people? If I were still trying to please people, I would not be a servant of Christ.

—Galatians 1:10

For the LORD *your God is living among you.*
He is a mighty savior.
He will take delight in you with gladness.
With his love, he will calm all your fears.
He will rejoice over you with joyful songs.

—Zephaniah 3:17 NLT

Funny people enjoy having me around because I will laugh at almost anything.

When my girls were in high school, they were both deeply involved in the theater department. Because dramatic teenagers are my absolute *favorite,* I took my role as drama mama seriously and spent almost as much time as they did hanging around the performing arts hallway at the high school. *Delight* is not a strong enough word to describe the way I still feel about the students, parents, and teachers who were part of that season of my life.

Despite the fact I proved quite useful to have around for selling tickets, gathering costumes, or locating a full-size coffin for a prop (true story), I was occasionally run off the premises during rehearsals because

I could not contain my laughter. During the final stages of preparation for their performance, although the student actors appreciated my encouragement, their teacher accused me of hampering the process by laughing at their antics too soon.

"They aren't funny yet! Quit laughing at them!"

In case you feel sorry for me, you will be happy to know that when opening night arrived, my obnoxiously loud laughter was once again welcomed, encouraged, and appreciated. I can't tell you how many times I heard, "Mrs. Johnson, we could hear you laughing!" as I congratulated students on another fabulous show. I'm not sure it is a marketable skill, but having a distinctive laugh has served me well as an enthusiastic drama mama and head cheerleader for the artsy kids.

Performers thrive on the positive reaction of their audience. Whether tears of tenderness, a gasp of surprise, a hearty belly laugh, or the coveted standing ovation at the final bow, when the cast and crew know they have connected with their audience, the many hours of hard work are worth the time and effort.

Recently I came across today's verse about choosing our audience. Since my youth group days, I have heard repeated counsel to perform for an "audience of one," instead of seeking to win the approval of many people. As a person who thrives on the accolades and affirmation of others, I often find this easier said than done. My love language is words of affirmation, and sometimes I find God's voice to be frustratingly quiet. Like many of the teachings of my faith, I understand and acknowledge the wisdom behind Paul's advice to the Galatians, but I often struggle to translate what I know into how I feel or how I choose to act.

However, one of the gifts of middle age is a gradual lessening of the hold other people's approval has over me. Perhaps this progress is due to the transforming work of the Holy Spirit in my life, but I suspect from talking to my other fifty-something friends it is also a function of exercising my "life is too short" muscle.

As I revisited the verse from Galatians, I realize I now see it through the lens of time and experience. Instead of a sigh of frustration over how far I fall short of this ideal, I thought about my drama mama years and what the word *audience* means for me now.

Is there a more perfect audience than a delighted parent?

In case you have not had the distinct pleasure of sitting in a theater or in the stands of a sporting event watching your child do what he or she loves best, the answer is an emphatic no. There is no more perfect audience than a delighted parent.

What if God is just that crazy about us?

What if the God who created the universe is sitting on the front row as we bravely step out of our comfort zone into the spotlight of our passion, holding His breath, leaning into our every word, and silently cheering us on until the moment He can jump to His feet cheering?

What if God wants us to succeed with every fiber of His being?

Perhaps we are encouraged to play to an audience of one instead of to the masses because the writers of Scripture knew God is our absolute, unabashedly, unashamedly, completely biased biggest fan. God knows how hard we worked. God knows how nervous we are. God knows how much we want to succeed. God sees us and He is completely *for* us.

Without meaning to do so, I once pictured God as a skeptical critic waiting for me to fail rather than as a delighted parent wanting me to succeed. Scripture is full of evidence to the contrary, so I decided to change my mind. There is no more perfect audience than our delighted Abba Father. He is crazy about us. He is our biggest fan. God sees our brave work, and He is on His feet cheering!

1. What does it mean to you to perform for an "audience of one"?
2. Our second verse talks about God delighting in us and rejoicing over us with songs. Close your eyes and picture what that might be like. What feelings or images come up for you?
3. If you think of God as a friendly and supportive audience, how does that change your willingness to take a risk? How might it make you braver?

Prayer: Abba Father, thank You for being my delighted parent. When I think about the things and people that bring me delight, I am humbled and moved to discover You feel that way about me. Thank You for always being on my side and cheering me on, even when I stumble. You are a good Father who loves me and wants me to pursue my dreams as I seek to serve You better and love You more. When I am tempted to give in to discouragement, let me hear You cheering me on from the audience. I love You too, Lord. Amen.

Being Brave Is Being Empowered by the Spirit

Day 34

All this I have spoken while still with you. But the Advocate, the Holy Spirit, whom the Father will send in my name, will teach you all things and will remind you of everything I have said to you. Peace I leave with you; my peace I give you. I do not give to you as the world gives. Do not let your hearts be troubled and do not be afraid.

—*John 14:25-27*

But you will receive power when the Holy Spirit comes on you; and you will be my witnesses in Jerusalem, and in all Judea and Samaria, and to the ends of the earth.

—*Acts 1:8*

Being brave is remembering we are not alone. Being brave is embracing the power available to us through Jesus.

People of faith have a secret weapon when it comes to being brave.

In the last days Jesus spent with His disciples during His earthly ministry, He tried to prepare them for the changes ahead. No matter how tenderly and patiently Jesus tried to explain, they struggled to grasp the realities of the circumstances heading their way. Although they traveled with Jesus and lived with Him for three years, although they saw Him work miracles time and again, much of what Jesus said to them in those final hours was still far beyond what they could absorb or comprehend.

On the night before He died, Jesus gathered with them to share the Passover supper. Before the evening meal was served, Jesus did something totally unexpected by getting up from the table, taking off His outer garment, and wrapping a towel around His waist. Jesus poured water into a basin and began to wash the dirty, dusty feet of His beloved disciples. One by one, He took the feet of each of the men into His hands and tenderly washed and dried each one. Just a few days before, they had seen their righteous and angry teacher turn over tables in the temple. Now Jesus knelt on the floor and performed the lowly work of a servant. As we talked about in Day 21, after He finished, Jesus told them this act of love was done as an example for them and they "should do as I have done for you" (John 13:15) going forward.

Jesus went on to share the meal and teach them about the new covenant and the deeper meaning of the bread and wine. Jesus asked them to remember Him each time they shared this meal in the future, and He spoke of His body being broken for them, His blood spilled for them. Jesus told them one of them would betray Him and turn Him over to the authorities. Jesus told them He would be leaving them soon, and He commanded them to love one another. Jesus said they would be known by the love they showed one another, and He told them they would do even greater things than He had done.

With each mention of His leaving, and each time Jesus did or said something unexpected or indecipherable, I'm certain the disciples grew more troubled. What in the world was Jesus saying? What would they do without Him? Could this possibly be true? How would they go on when Jesus wasn't there to lead them, teach them, love them, and guide them? How would they ever remember these strange, terrible, wonderful, confusing things Jesus said? What did it all mean?

Finally, Jesus promised He would not leave them orphans when He went back to the Father. Although Jesus would no longer be with them in the flesh, He would ask the Father to send them another counselor who will be with them forever and help them understand all they have heard. He would send the Advocate, the Spirit described in today's verses.

After Jesus's resurrection, they finally understand. Just like the disciples in the room with Jesus that night, for all of us who accept the gift Jesus offers, the Holy Spirit is our inheritance, our birthright, and our promise. Through the power and presence of the Holy Spirit—the one who Jesus calls Counselor, Comforter, and Advocate—we are offered an unbreakable connection to the divine. Scripture repeatedly entreats us to be strong, courageous, and unafraid because God is with us. The gift of the Holy Spirit is the tangible fulfillment of that promise. As we plug in to the power and presence of Spirit, we are given the tools we need to experience the power and peace of God.

Being empowered by the Spirit is essential on the path to being brave.

1. As you imagine that last night with Jesus, what question would you have asked Him if you had been one of the disciples?
2. How would you describe the Holy Spirit to someone who is unfamiliar with the concept?
3. In what ways have you experienced the power of the Holy Spirit in your life?

Prayer: Father, what a gift You have given us in the indwelling of the Holy Spirit! As Your children, we know the Holy Spirit is part of our inheritance, a gift You freely give to those who love You and call You Lord. Show us the way to fully access the power and peace available to us through Your Spirit so that we will show the fruit of that Spirit to the world. You don't leave us alone. Remind us that You are with us always and that, through Your Spirit, we have all we need. Show us how to be brave through the power of Your Holy Spirit. Amen.

Day 35

If any of you lacks wisdom, you should ask God, who gives generously to all without finding fault, and it will be given to you.

—*James 1:5*

I keep asking that the God of our Lord Jesus Christ, the glorious Father, may give you the Spirit of wisdom and revelation, so that you may know him better.

—*Ephesians 1:17*

Several years ago, I learned about a program—a lay counseling program to assist the pastoral staff with the needs of people hurting within our community—I thought we should offer at the church I attended. I read all the literature available and believed it fit perfectly with the needs and resources of our congregation at the time. And I believed I would be a perfect match to be part of the program once the administrators got it started. I began praying for the staff and leadership of our church, believing God would make it happen in His perfect timing.

And I waited. And I prayed. And then I waited some more.

Clearly, *those* people were not listening to God's directives! *Someone* needed to start this essential program—the program I couldn't get off my mind, the program that stirred my heart and quickened my pulse. Why weren't these people paying attention to this obvious need and the clear solution to that need? Someone needed to *do* something!

I'm sure you already see where this is going.

After several months of thinking and praying about the program and wondering why no one was following through on what seemed so obvious to me, the identity of the mysterious "someone" became clear. Although I didn't hear an audible voice confirming my role, one day I clearly understood the reason why this program had been haunting me. I was the "someone" who needed to do something. The assignment was mine.

Still somewhat fearful and unsure, I went to see my pastor the next day. We had the program up and running within the year.

Since this experience, I have learned to listen more carefully when my imagination is captured or when I find myself drawn to a project or an assignment. When I am seeking God's presence regularly in prayer, I gain clarity in the ways I am called to engage in the world. I hear God's whispers and nudges as an invitation to explore where I might have a role to play in the work God is doing in the world. Perhaps, as in the situation above, I am being invited to partner with God in a way I had not previously considered.

However, as I seek to do my part, I am also learning to check in regularly with God and the goals I have previously identified as priorities so I am not spreading myself too thin or wasting time on efforts better left to others more suited to the task. Not every good cause is *my* good cause; not every worthy battle is mine to fight. Learning to say no is every bit as important as learning to say yes. For me, the only way to choose my yes or no with any integrity is by checking in with the One who sees the big picture in ways I cannot.

Scripture repeatedly invites us to pray for wisdom, with the understanding God is more than happy to answer that prayer in the affirmative. When we are curious about why something has been on our mind, we can go to God with our wondering. The person we can't get off our mind, the need that always brings a lump to our throat, the interest or hobby we are drawn to repeatedly but haven't made time to try—perhaps these are the ways the Holy Spirit invites us to reach out, sign up, and be brave. Trusting our heart and listening to our Father, the path becomes clear.

1. Was there an experience that came to mind while you were reading this story? Have you had a similar experience where you felt a tug at your heart to step out of your comfort zone and do something new?
2. How do you know when something is your assignment? How do you make choices between the many good things on which you could choose to spend your time?
3. Have you ever prayed for wisdom on a particular issue? If so, how has God answered your prayer?

Prayer: Father, who is always at work, show us where we can sign up to join You. Help us learn to recognize Your voice in our spirit; and, when we hear You calling, give us the courage to say YES! Remind us how important it is to talk with You every day through prayer and Scripture. Only through regular communication with You can we begin to recognize the sound of Your voice. Don't give up on us when we get scared, but remind us You are always right by our side. As we abide in You, all things are possible. Amen.

Day 36

When you are put into their hands, do not worry what you will say or how you will say it. The words will be given you when the time comes. It will not be you who will speak the words. The Spirit of your Father will speak through you.

—Matthew 10:19-20 NLV

At that time the Holy Spirit will teach you what you must say.

—Luke 12:12 NCV

I prepared for weeks. I volunteered to give the message at our church's annual women's Christmas event, my first time to speak to the women of my church in this type of setting. I wanted desperately to offer something meaningful to our group. I chose a topic, did the work, prepared my notes, and practiced in front of the mirror to make sure I didn't go over the allotted time. And I prayed. "Please, Lord, use my words to be a blessing. Give me Your Spirit. Help me do a good job for my friends."

The evening of the event finally arrived and I was nervous but excited. I prayed before I went inside and again before I began to speak. As I started to speak, I felt a sense of peace and purpose along with the nervousness. God was with me and one way or another, even though I was scared, all would be well.

After my talk, a woman who was new to our church came up to me with tears streaming down her face. Through her tears, she shared with me how a particular insight I shared had touched her heart: "What you said felt like it was just for me. Like God was sending me a message to offer healing in a place where I have been hurting for a long time. I can't thank you enough for what you said."

I stood there in shock and awe. The exact item she mentioned had *not* been in my prepared notes. This particular topic had never occurred to me in my hours of preparation. I hadn't planned it and was somewhat surprised when it popped out of my mouth while I was speaking, a passing moment of inspiration and insight that I threw in at the last moment.

Indeed, the thing she needed to hear most of all in the world was a gift straight from God, not from me.

As believers, we are each promised the gift of the Holy Spirit. Jesus promised He would send the Comforter to remind us of all He had taught. We are not stumbling through our days alone. As we learn to rely on His guidance, we begin to recognize those moments of insight and inspiration as gifts of grace. An inspired word of comfort to a hurting friend, a reminder of a phone call of encouragement we wanted to make, the answer to a seemingly overwhelming problem with which we have been struggling—all evidence of the kindness and compassion of our Abba Father meeting us in our moment of need. As we lean in and listen, the whispers grow louder, and we begin to trust the still small voice within us is a voice worthy of our attention. This voice is our truest self in connection and communication with our Maker.

1. Have you experienced a time when you felt the Holy Spirit gave you the words you needed? If not, would you be willing to pray for inspiration in a situation you are currently facing?
2. What is the difference between intuition and the whisper of the Holy Spirit?
3. Does the idea that the Holy Spirit is with you and wants to empower you make you braver? What might you be willing to do differently, if you believed it was true?

Prayer: Gracious Father, we are amazed by the ways You equip us and prepare us for whatever we face. Give us words to say in the difficult situation we are dreading, give us patience to endure the hard task, and inspire us to bring moments of beauty and grace into the world as we go through our days. Give us a taste of Your Spirit so we begin to crave Your presence in every part of our life. Fill us, Lord, and let us point others to You. Amen.

Day 37

If you spend yourselves in behalf of the hungry
and satisfy the needs of the oppressed,
then your light will rise in the darkness,
and your night will become like the noonday.
The Lord will guide you always;
he will satisfy your needs in a sun-scorched land
and will strengthen your frame.
You will be like a well-watered garden,
like a spring whose waters never fail.

—Isaiah 58:10-11

He has shown you, O mortal, what is good.
And what does the Lord require of you?
To act justly and to love mercy
and to walk humbly with your God.

—Micah 6:8

Dave is the director of The Lamb Center, our local day shelter for homeless and poor individuals. Just like Jesus, Dave loves people just as they are and offers them radical hospitality. He is gentle, kind, and patient, but he knows how to set firm loving boundaries when needed. Dave makes sure hungry people are fed and strangers feel welcome. Dave sees every person he meets, no matter their situation, as a child of God trying to find his or her way home. A recovering alcoholic himself, Dave first came to the shelter sixteen years ago when he was in the early stages of recovery and was required to do community service. Eventually, he grew to understand how much God loved him and, out of the grace he had been given, found his calling in loving and serving the poor and poor in spirit.

Since I began serving weekly at The Lamb Center, I have been stretched. Initially, I was overwhelmed by my sense of inadequacy in the face of such great need. I was moved and humbled by the stories of the people I met around the Bible study table each week, yet what could I do to help? What did a suburban mom have to offer someone living in the desperate circumstances many of these folks found themselves in?

So I watched Dave and tried to do what he did. Over time, I discovered his secret. Simply put, Dave gives the guests at The Lamb Center the gift of himself.

Just like Dave, I have myself to give. With the help of the Holy Spirit, I can offer my friends at the shelter my love, my listening ear, the touch of my hand, a warm hug, a moment of prayer, or a kind word. I have my unique life experiences to offer—the losses I have survived, the pain I have felt, the joy of knowing God, and the wisdom of following Him. I have my love of God's word to share and the knowledge that the promises within are for every single one of us, regardless of our circumstances, our resources, or our past.

I have me to offer, a gift no one else can give.

As I think about giving the gift of self, I am touched and inspired by the tenderness of the relationship between Jesus and John, often called the beloved disciple. Throughout John's Gospel account, he repeatedly referred to himself as "the disciple whom Jesus loved" (see John 13:23). We see evidence of this deep affection in the stories John told about sticking close to Jesus in the last days and hours of Jesus's ministry on earth. In the upper room for their last meal together, John reclined against Jesus, hanging on His every word. One translation describes him as having his head on Jesus's shoulder (John 13:22-25 MSG). In the final moments before Jesus died, John was the only disciple who stood resolutely with the women at the foot of the cross. Seeing his faithfulness, Jesus entrusted His mother Mary into John's care (John 19:26-27).

Finally, after hearing the news of Jesus's resurrection from the women, John and Peter raced to the empty tomb. In his account, John mentioned twice that he, not Peter, arrived first to find the tomb empty, clearly eager to show his longing to see Jesus and perhaps highlight his athletic prowess (John 20:3-8). Because John loved Jesus and believed with all his heart that Jesus loved him, John didn't hesitate to offer all that he was and all that he had—body, mind, and spirit—trusting Jesus would lead the way.

After serving ten years at the shelter, I've learned lessons from this community that have changed the way I live the other six days of the week. Although the challenges we face as individuals might be different, we each have the same need to know our story matters and we are not alone. Like my friends at the shelter, I'm learning to be vulnerable, to ask for help, and to share my struggles openly and honestly. Whether at the shelter, in my neighborhood, or in my own home, I remember the deep healing God brings when we feed hungry people, listen to lonely people, and pray with those who are hurting.

And I remember, as I remind my friends each week at the shelter, I too am God's beloved and He will never leave me. So, like John and like my friends at The Lamb Center, I remember to follow Jesus closely and do the next right thing, one day at a time, one moment at a time. A task made much easier when we stick together and give one another the simple, yet profound, gift of ourselves.

1. Think about the ways you give the gift of yourself in your home and community. How might you be brave and stretch yourself one step further?
2. What are the practical ways we access the power of the Holy Spirit to do things we might not do alone? What spiritual disciplines (prayer, Scripture, worship, service) draw you closer to Spirit and make you braver?
3. What do you think about "the gift of presence"? Do you think just being there and available to someone who is hurting is enough? Why or why not?

Prayer: Loving Father, open our eyes to the people around us who are hurting and in need of the gift of encouragement. Help us be brave five minutes longer and perhaps reach out to someone with whom we might not normally connect. A smile, a kind word, a compliment, or an offer to help might make all the difference in someone's day. Nudge us, bring someone to mind, give us an idea, speak to us through Your Spirit, and show us how we can be part of bringing Your kingdom closer simply by offering the gift of our self. Amen.

Day 38

Trust in the LORD with all your heart
and lean not on your own understanding;
in all your ways submit to him,
and he will make your paths straight.

—Proverbs 3:5-6

Rejoice always, pray without ceasing, give thanks in all circumstances; for this is the will of God in Christ Jesus for you.

—1 Thessalonians 5:16-18 ESV

Some of the best moments of my life have been marked by the decision to hold hands and pray.

One of the places where I have learned the most about holding hands and praying is The Lamb Center. At The Lamb Center, we experience the presence of the Holy Spirit by holding hands to pray at least six times a day as a community. We pause, we gather, we join hands, and we bow our heads. We talk to God about what has happened so far in our day and what is coming next. We acknowledge how much we need our heavenly Father and how much we need each other. We say thank you, and we ask for help. No fancy words or rituals, just a moment to say, "We love You too, Lord."

In this community, prayer is a part of the moment-by-moment rhythm of each day, as natural as breathing. If I'm honest, this kind of "praying without ceasing" is a way of living to which I have always aspired personally but have never been able to maintain consistently on my own.

One of my favorite times of prayer at The Lamb Center occurred a few years ago. In June 2016, after years of waiting and hoping, we celebrated the completion of our beautiful brand-new facility with an enormous grand-opening party. More than four hundred people wandered through the building that day and took tours of the place that God had built in answer to thousands of prayers. Community leaders spoke, we cut a red ribbon with giant scissors, and we took hundreds of pictures. It was a day brimming with joy, laughter, and gratitude.

Two years before, after many years of prayerfully searching for the right place, our Lamb Center community boldly and faithfully set out to raise $4.5 million to build a more welcoming place of respite for poor and homeless individuals in our community. When the grand opening party started that Sunday, we were joyfully celebrating the fact that God had already provided $4 million toward our goal through the generosity and prayers of His people, an amount beyond our wildest dreams. When the party ended, as if all the above wasn't enough, we found out that someone had agreed to pay the final balance on the building. In answer to years of praying, God provided all $4.5 million, and the building was paid for in full within a few months. Without a mortgage, we have been able to pour ongoing donations into expanded services for our guests. As we held hands and prayed our closing prayer of gratitude the day of the party, I was not the only one in tears.

So what is the message here? If we hold hands and pray six times a day, God will give us $4.5 million and the desires of our heart?

Not really. But maybe?

Holding hands and praying together is full of hard things like humility, vulnerability, intimacy, and expectations. We admit we don't have all the answers and we need help. We acknowledge our lack of control and our reliance on things much bigger than ourselves, both God and the power of community. We let down our guard and we take off our masks of superiority, pride, and independence. We can't see what is coming when we bow our heads and close our eyes. As we widen our circle, we discover some of our hands are a little bit dirty or sweaty or freezing cold. Sometimes, holding hands and praying together can be uncomfortable or awkward.

Yet, every single time I hold hands and pray with someone else, I experience the tangible presence of God in a way I don't always experience when I pray alone. Although there is never a wrong time to pray, we might reach out our hand and humble our hearts to pray:

- while gathered at the table about to share a meal with people we love;
- before heading out to serve for the day in the community;
- while preparing to go on a field, a stage, or into a meeting with my team;
- after being served with coffee or wine in a friend's living room;
- while begging God for healing and answers in the face of illness, anger, tragedy, or grief.

Whatever the setting, we are changed when we dare to hold hands and pray. Holy and profound things happen when we hold hands and pray. Healing and transformation happen when we hold hands and pray.

Miracles happen when we hold hands and pray.

1. Do you find it difficult to pray with other people? Why or why not?
2. How does God show up differently when we pray with other people? Or how do we experience God differently?
3. If someone asked you to share a tangible answer to prayer, what is the first story that pops into your mind? How did that answer to prayer change you?

Prayer: God of community, in Scripture, You repeatedly invite us to come to You in prayer. Alone or together, we are invited to come to You with the desires of our heart. We are grateful for Your willingness to hear our prayers, and we are blown away by the ways in which You answer those prayers. Help us be humble enough to bow our heads, join hands, and acknowledge Your power and presence. You love us so much, Lord, and we know You want to bring us good things. You alone hold the key to the future. We are in good hands when we remember to hold hands and pray. Amen.

Day 39

I love you, Lord, my strength.
The Lord is my rock, my fortress and my deliverer;
my God is my rock, in whom I take refuge,
my shield and the horn of my salvation, my stronghold.
I call to the Lord, who is worthy of praise,
and I have been saved from my enemies.

—Psalm 18:1-3

When he saw Peter and John about to enter, he asked them for money. Peter looked straight at him, as did John. Then Peter said, "Look at us!" So the man gave them his attention, expecting to get something from them. Then Peter said, "Silver or gold I do not have, but what I do have I give you. In the name of Jesus Christ of Nazareth, walk."

—Acts 3:3-6

I will never forget her words and the enthusiasm with which she spoke, tears in her eyes:

"God is real! This is all real! It is all true! He is *so* good!"

We began our Bible study at The Lamb Center discussing adoration: the practice of expressing our love to the Lord. As we read the first few verses of Psalm 18, we talked about the intimacy of the way David repeated the word *my* over and over. David had clearly experienced the presence of God. For David, this God was *real* and this God was *his*.

In attendance that day was a young woman named Angela who was new to The Lamb Center. Angela was there with her three small children, all under the age of four. As we spoke, Angela expertly and lovingly cared for her babies: rocking one to sleep, offering Play-Doh to keep another busy, finding a snack for another. As we spoke about David's personal God, Angela listened carefully and then asked this question: "Is there a time that *we* had experienced God in such a way that we knew He was real? Did those of us around the table have a story about a time we knew God was really there?"

This question opened up a time of sharing that I will treasure forever. It wasn't a large group, but each of us shared a time when God reached down into our lives and made Himself known in a personal, intimate way. Most everyone shared, some in more detail than others. Truly, as is often the case at The Lamb Center, it wasn't always clear who was a guest, a volunteer, or staff as we passed around the tissue box and wiped away our tears of gratitude for the gracious God we had each met. Those worldly barriers meant very little as we shared our unique experiences of God's unexpected, intimate, gentle, comforting, encouraging hand in our lives.

There was one story with which Angela seemed to be particularly interested. My friend Marie shared her story of a time when she was living, in her words, in a "very dark place." She had gotten herself into a particularly difficult financial circumstance and was in danger of losing the one thing that meant the most to her—the one thing that kept her connected to the daughter she cherished. In this desperate circumstance, she asked a stranger for money. He gave Marie a few dollars, but then he offered her something even more meaningful. He laid out his Bible on the hood of his car, took her hands in his, and told her God saw her, loved her, and was on her side. Eventually, he led her in a prayer of surrender to Jesus, even though she had told the man she was "not really into Jesus." He told her it was okay to go to Jesus with all her reservations, all her doubts, all her skepticism.

From that moment forward, her life has been transformed. Slowly, one baby step at a time, she began to trust God to lead her out of her circumstances. Like the beggar at the temple gate, she has experienced healing beyond what she had originally asked. Marie begged for money and received new life. As Marie told Angela the many concrete, personal ways that God had redeemed her life, tears ran down Marie's face and she said these powerful words: "God is real! This is all real! It is all true! God is *so* good!"

As I told her after the Bible study that day, Marie was now getting to experience one of the great joys of Kingdom living. By sharing what God has done in her life, Marie has the privilege of blessing another person: an opportunity to give back a portion of what she had been given. The same is true for each of us. God blesses us so we can be a blessing to someone else. I experience God's love more deeply when I share His love with someone else. I understand the depth of my love for God as I see God at work in the lives of His people. As I see someone else discover the God I love, I fall in love with Him all over again. Although I sometimes feel God's presence and power in my moments alone with Him, I almost always feel God's presence and power in moments of authentic community. We are not meant to walk this journey alone;

God wired us to live in community and to encourage one another as we love and serve Him with our whole heart.

My friend, have you heard the good news?

God is real! It is all true! God is so *good!*

1. If someone asked you to share a time you knew God was real, what story would you tell?
2. How does sharing your story of God's faithfulness empower you to trust God even more? How does it make you braver?
3. Divide your life into decades. For each decade, list at least three times you see God's presence in your life during that time frame. Thank God for His faithfulness in being with you on every step of your journey to this point.

Prayer: Faithful, timeless God, thank You for Your perfect love that drives out fear. Remind us when we feel alone that You are on our side. Powerful God, You are MY strength, MY rock, MY fortress, and MY deliverer, yet You show up for each of us in just the way we need. You are our Abba Father who fights for us. Give us boldness when given the opportunity to share the ways in which You are working in each of our lives. You are real, it's all true, and You are so good! Amen.

Day 40

What, then, shall we say in response to these things? If God is for us, who can be against us?

—Romans 8:31

That is what is meant by the Scriptures which say that no mere man has ever seen, heard, or even imagined what wonderful things God has ready for those who love the Lord. But we know about these things because God has sent his Spirit to tell us, and his Spirit searches out and shows us all of God's deepest secrets.

—1 Corinthians 2:9-10 TLB

As I write this, I'm looking at the bluest water I have ever seen. We are on a family trip in the Caribbean, a place I have never visited before. A tiny lizard runs by and stops to look up at me curiously for a moment before he heads off into the lush vegetation surrounding my quiet bench near the ocean. I've seen photos and videos of water this color, a turquoise-azure-aqua mixture, but the reality is far beyond what I imagined. I've taken photo after photo trying to capture the beauty of the sunlight sparkling on the water, as if I could somehow pack the view in my suitcase to enjoy later at home, even though I know firsthand the limitations of a photo representation.

Like my ocean photo versus the reality, once we have experienced life empowered by God's Spirit, anything less becomes a cheap substitute, a filmy out-of-focus representation of the possibility for more. The adventure of stepping bravely into the unknown, trusting in divine guidance, and believing our story is a worthy and necessary part of a larger story awakens the part of us we never knew was asleep. Connection to a good, loving, trustworthy God and connection to a community who names us brave becomes the way we choose; it is the way we were designed to live, a return to the garden we didn't know we were missing. We intentionally turn down the volume of our inner critic and turn up the volume on the voice of our gift-giving creative Father. We refuse to hustle, compare, and compete for our worthiness any longer and choose instead to celebrate our unique journey, offering it with open hands and heart to a hurting world. We try new things, embrace progress instead of perfection, and enjoy the process of discovery called growing up. We gently extend grace and forgiveness to others and most especially, finally, to ourselves.

This new life is beautiful in a deeper, richer, more colorful way than life before. When we begin to dig deeper for courage, we find courage has been there all along, waiting to be summoned. Everything we have needed was right there, and we are surprised to discover we were already brave. We have always been brave; we just needed to be reminded.

Once we remember we are brave, we can no longer hide from ourselves and others. Being scared is no longer an excuse, and someday is a myth. Now is the time; this is the moment. Following Jesus is the adventure for which we have been waiting.

Listen carefully for the better voice beckoning us toward the next right thing.

- Be strong and courageous, and do the work. Do not be afraid or discouraged, for the LORD God, my God, is with you (1 Chronicles 28:20).
- "For God has not given us a spirit of fear and timidity, but of power, love, and self-discipline" (2 Timothy 1:7 NLT).
- "On the day I called, You answered me. / You made me bold with strength in my soul" (Psalm 138:3 TLV).
- "And we know that God causes everything to work together for the good of those who love God and are called according to his purpose for them" (Romans 8:28 NLT).

Where do we go from here? What else is the better voice saying to you? Writer and pastor Frederick Buechner describes our next step like this: "The place God calls you to is the place where your deep gladness and the world's deep hunger meet."[1]

Now that you have remembered how brave you are, where is God calling you?

1. What is the most significant thing you have learned about yourself in the past forty days?
2. What one thing would you want others to know about being brave?
3. Write a letter of invitation to you from God. What is God inviting you to do next? What does God want you to know about how He feels about you and what He desires for you? If you listen closely, what do you hear Him saying?

Prayer: Strong Father, I am brave! When I forget again, and I will, remind me of the spirit You have given me—a spirit of power, love, and self-discipline. Help me be bold, resilient, authentic, and vulnerable. Show me where and how to engage the world, knowing I am empowered by Your brave Spirit. I say YES! Amen.

Note

1. Frederick Buechner, *Wishful Thinking: A Seeker's ABC* (New York: HarperOne, 1993), 95.

Being Brave Invitation from God

My Beloved Child–

Your voice matters. I made you in such a way that no one else has been or will ever be just like you. You are unique, like all my children, and that makes you special. You already have everything you need to live a great big life full of adventure, love, sacrifice, meaning, and purpose.

You don't need anything else to be ready. Someday is a myth. No one is ever ready. Everything you have experienced, suffered, and learned up to this point is all part of the masterpiece we are making together. I gave you gifts and passions that only you can use to make the world a better place. Don't waste these gifts I have given you on a small, safe, comfortable life. I have never once told my children to play it safe.

Don't let the voices of doubt, fear, or shame keep you paralyzed. They are lies. You will make mistakes, but I will be there with you every step of the way. Struggling is part of the journey and helps you grow stronger, so don't give up when life gets hard. Deeper roots produce richer, more beautiful fruit. Cultivate resilience and be willing to learn a new dance. Dream big and love bigger, trusting I am with you and will never leave you.

Share what I have given you with others. Tell people about the

Kingdom. Try something new, and, if you fail, don't be afraid to try again. Love people who are hard to love and listen to them. Be real, authentic, and vulnerable. People will still love you, even when you drop the act. If they don't, bless them and walk away.

I see your heart, and I know you love me too. We are in this together, so don't be afraid. My plan for your life is for you to pursue your passions and use them to make the world a little better and remind people that they are loved. I'm not that concerned about the specific details as long as you live in grace and walk in love. Don't wait. Do the work. Trust the process. Obey even when you are scared. Follow me and do the next right thing.

Are you ready for an adventure? Let's get started!

I love you.

–God

Scriptures About Fear and Courage

Deuteronomy 3:22
Deuteronomy 31:6
Joshua 1:7-9
1 Chronicles 28:20
Psalm 23
Psalm 27:1
Psalm 31:24
Psalm 34:4
Psalm 46
Psalm 56:3-4
Psalm 91:1-16
Psalm 94:19
Psalm 118
Proverbs 3:5-6
Isaiah 35:4
Isaiah 41:10-13
Isaiah 43:1
Isaiah 54:4
Zephaniah 3:17
Matthew 6:34
Matthew 10:28
Mark 6:50
Luke 12:22-26
John 14:27
Romans 8:15
Romans 8:38-39
1 Corinthians 15:58
1 Corinthians 16:13
Ephesians 6:10
Philippians 1:12-14
Philippians 4:4-7
2 Timothy 1:7
Hebrews 13:5-6
1 Peter 3:14-16
1 Peter 5:6-7
1 John 4:18

Thank you for taking the Being Brave *forty-day journey with me. I would love to hear about the brave adventures you and God are embarking on now that you remember you are brave! Join our* Being Brave *community and tell us your story at my website: www.kellyiveyjohnson.com.*

During our journey, I introduced you to The Lamb Center and the work they are doing with homeless and poor individuals in the Washington, D.C., suburbs. If you would like to know more about their ministry, please visit their website at www.thelambcenter.org.